HOW TO PREPARE
SERMONS

HOW TO PREPARE SERMONS

(Revised)

By

WILLIAM EVANS, Ph.D., D.D., Litt.D.
Former Teacher at Moody Bible Institute

MOODY PRESS

CHICAGO

37 Printing/EE/Year 88 87 86 85

Printed in the United States of America

FOREWORD

THIS VOLUME is not an attempt to present a complete and exhaustive treatment on homiletics—the science and art of preaching—for there are already on the market larger and more comprehensive works on the subject. This book is prepared not only for theological students but also to supply the need of those who find themselves denied the privileges of a regular ministerial training but who, nevertheless, feel called upon to preach or proclaim the Gospel of the Lord Jesus Christ. Indeed, the lectures herein printed are in substance the same as delivered to young men and women preparing themselves for Christian service in a Bible school. This fact accounts for their conversational style, which the author has not deemed wise to change.

Christian laymen, even though not preachers in the accepted sense of that term, desiring to be able to prepare brief Gospel messages and Bible readings will find the help they need in this volume. Those seeking help in the preparation of talks for young people's societies, conventions, clubs and so on may receive hints and suggestions in this work.

The book contains theory and practice. Part I deals with the methods of constructing various kinds of sermons and Bible messages. Part II is composed of outlines illustrating Part I.

The closing chapter of Part I on "Illustrations and Their Use" has been found so helpful wherever delivered that it is thought advisable to give it a place in this volume.

WILLIAM EVANS

CONTENTS

PART II

Outlines of Sermons, Gospel Messages, and Bible Readings

PART I

Chapter 1

DEFINITIONS

I. HOMILETICS

THE WORD "homiletics" is derived from the Greek word *homilia* and signifies either a mutual talk and conversation or a set discourse. The preachers in the early Church were in the habit of calling their public discourses "talks," thus making it proper to speak of what is in the present day in some quarters called a "gospel talk."

From the word *homilia* has come the English word "homiletics," which has reference to that science or art— or indeed both—which deals with the structure of Christian discourse, embracing all that pertains to the preparation and delivery of sermons and Bible addresses. It shows us how to prepare a sermon or Gospel address and how to deliver it effectually. Homiletics, then, is the art and science of preaching.

II. WHAT IS PREACHING?*

Preaching is the proclamation of the Good News of salvation through man to men. Its two constituent elements are a man and a message—*personality* and *truth*. The Gospel proclaimed by means of the written page or the printed book is not preaching. There is no such thing as seeing "sermons in stones." Again, the proclamation of any kind of message other than the gospel message, which

*Cf. Phillips Brooks, *Preaching*.

is the truth of God as revealed in the Bible and especially
in Jesus Christ, is not preaching. Much of what is heard
from so-called Christian pulpits of today is not real preaching. The discussion of politics, popular authors, current
topics, and kindred themes may rightfully be called addresses, and may result in the emulation of the orator, but
such efforts can in no sense of the word be called preaching; and such men have absolutely no right, so long as they
continue to deliver such addresses from the pulpit, to the
honored name of preachers of the Gospel. The message
of the very truth of God through man to men—that is
preaching.

III. WHAT IS A PREACHER?

The preacher is separated by God for the specific work
of preaching the Gospel and is a man who from one side
of his nature takes in the truth from God and from the
other side gives out that truth to men. He deals with God
in behalf of men; he deals with men in behalf of God.

This truth must not be mechanically expressed. It must
not be merely truth through the mouth, over the lips, in
the intellect, or by means of the pen, but truth through
his character and personality. Every fiber of the man's
moral and spiritual nature must be controlled by the truth.
The force of a blow is measured not by the arm only, but
also by the weight of the body behind the arm. And just
here is the difference men instinctively feel between one
preacher and another. The hearer is persuaded that the
truth which is being proclaimed from the pulpit has come
over one preacher, whereas it has come through the other.
Consequently, the preaching of the one is tame and uninteresting, while that of the other is strong, fascinating,
and convincing.

The preacher must not be a mere machine, an automaton; he must be a real man—a good man, full of the Holy Spirit and faith. The effect of such a life and such preaching will be that many people will be added to the Lord (Acts 11:24).

The personality of the preacher has very much to do with the effectiveness of his message. An artist may be a profligate and yet produce a picture or a statue which will call forth the admiration of the people; an author may be dissolute in morals and yet produce a book that will set the world aflame with his popularity. These are works of art and can be considered apart from the man himself. But not so with the preacher and his sermon; it is a part of himself; indeed, it must be the expression of his very life and experience. If such is not the case, then what is called preaching will be nothing but "sounding brass, or a tinkling cymbal."

Personality counts in preaching. Is this not one of the reasons why many sermons do not usually make good reading? The personality of the preacher is absent. Of course, there are some very splendid exceptions to this fact, but often—alas, very often—the sermon is but an echo of the man. Have we not wondered more than once at the dryness of a sermon we were reading when at the time we heard it we were moved to the very depths of our being? What was lacking? The personality of the preacher, that is all—but how much is wrapped up in that personality!

The experience of the truth must be in the preacher himself before he can proclaim it with convicting force in and through the sermon. Given a man who is a born artist, you have only to supply the palette and brush, or chisel and mallet with mere technical skill, and you have a statue or a picture. And if you have your preacher—a man with the experience of the truth in him—you will find that very little else is needed to set free the sermon in him.

From this it is clearly evident that true preparation for the Gospel ministry does not consist in mere tricks in sermon-making or delivery, but in the development of true personality. Such a man in the pulpit will surely prove to be a preacher who will reach the masses.

We hear complaints on every hand to the effect that people do not want Gospel preaching today. This is a mistake. There never was a day when people wanted it more than now. What they do object to is a Gospel read or declaimed and not preached. In other words, they ask for a consecrated personality in the pulpit. Look abroad today, and what do you see? Wherever the Gospel is preached by a consecrated personality, there are found men and women to hear it.

Chapter 2

PERSONALITY OF THE PREACHER

It has been said that truth and personality are the fundamentals of all true preaching. With reference to truth it is hardly necessary for the content of the message to be considered here except to say that it must be the truth of God as it is revealed in our Lord and Saviour Jesus Christ— that truth which is fitted for every man, and changes not with the passing of the years.

This chapter deals with the preacher and the development of his personality. What kind of man ought the preacher to be? What elements in his character need to be emphasized in the development of personality if he is to be a real success in the ministry of the Gospel?

I. HE MUST NOT BE AN IMITATOR

Such a statement might seem to be altogether unnecessary were it not for the fact that the average preacher is actually almost anyone else except himself. Every truth the preacher expresses and every message he delivers ought to be stamped with his own personality and should be expressed in his own way.

Let us remember that God has made no two faces or voices alike. Each man has his own individuality to stamp on the work which God has given him to do. If your name is David, and you are called upon to kill your Goliath, then

do not covet the armor of Saul, but take your sling and
stone, and by the help of God the boasting giant will fall
and lick the dust. Many a man has failed in his ministry,
when otherwise he would have been a glorious success,
simply because he was not willing to take himself as God
made him. The very individuality with which God has
endowed us is the very thing which makes us worth hearing—otherwise a phonograph could do the work about as
well and at less expense.

It is worth noticing that men who copy the ways and
manners of other preachers who have been successful
almost always copy their faults, not their virtues, and in
the attempt to do so become ridiculous in the extreme.
What ludicrous results may be observed when men imitate
with servility the doings of others! The ambitious young
preacher who is aspiring to be a genius copies the pecu-
liarities in attitude and manner of the popular preacher
near him and causes actual merriment in the very matters
in which he thinks he is most effective. Such a preacher is
much like those monkeys whose imitative power, Harris
says, the Indians turn to destruction in this way: Coming
to their haunts with basins full of water or honey, they
wash their faces in the sight of these animals, and then,
substituting pots of thin glue instead of the water or honey,
they retire out of sight. The monkeys, as soon as the Indians are gone, come down and wash their faces likewise
and, sticking their eyelids together, become blind and are
easily captured. In other places the Indians bring their
boots into the woods and, putting them on and off, leave
them well lined with glue or a sort of birdlime, so that
when the unhappy monkeys put them on, the boots stick
fast and hinder their escape. How many men have found
it impossible to extricate themselves from difficulties into

which they have been drawn through attempting to imitate others.

By shining in the light of others we may have made a name as great preachers; our people may have eulogized us. But we must turn now from imitating others and become our own true selves.

The preacher should be himself, his best self, his consecrated self, his highest self. In so doing he will best prove his sincerity, honor his God, and become a means of greatest blessing to the people to whom he ministers.

II. HE SHOULD BE A MAN OF DEEP PIETY

Again and again in his letters to the young preacher Timothy, the aged Apostle Paul insists on purity and piety of life. The great and often the only difference in many sermons is simply the difference in the character of the preachers. To know the inner life of such men as Spurgeon, Moody, or Finney is to understand the secret of their powerful ministry. What we are does indeed speak louder than what we say and certainly is more effective in the long run. A bad man cannot long remain undiscovered in the ministry. If the preacher is not living up to his preaching, the people will soon find it out—then woe be to that man. "Be ye clean, that bear the vessels of the LORD."

The preacher must be clean in the habits of his life. Little foxes spoil the vines. He must have no impure habits nor secret vices. God will openly put to shame him who secretly sins. David's life is an illustration of this truth (II Sam. 12:12). Paul's exhortation to Timothy is still a helpful one: "Flee youthful lusts." The preacher will be shorn of his power in the pulpit if he is not clean in his private life. He cannot face his people with confidence if he knows that his life is not pure as it ought to be. The very confidence of the people will rebuke his hypocrisy. The preacher must cleanse himself from all defilement of the flesh and spirit, perfecting holiness in the fear of the Lord. If a man shall purge himself, he shall be a vessel unto honor, meet and prepared for the Master's use.

The preacher must also be truthful. Exaggeration is lying, stretching the truth is lying, and a lie in the pulpit is worse than a lie anywhere else. If an illustration which the preacher is using did not occur in his own life, then he must not say it did. How many a preacher has been conscious that the story he was telling while in the pulpit was not true, that he was exaggerating, yes, that he was actually lying. He must not do evil that good may come from it.

A preacher's life may be a lie; he may be pretending to be in life what he is not in reality. Piety in the pulpit must be accompanied by piety in the home. A certain quality of life is expected from the preacher by his people, and reasonably so, too; he must see to it he proves himself worthy of their confidence. He must tell the truth to God. If he has vowed to Him, he must keep his vows. He must tell the truth to men. If he has promised to meet an obligation on a certain day, he must meet it; and if he is unable to meet it at the proper time, be a man and go and confess his inability to do so.

III. HE MUST BE A MAN OF GRAVITY

He should consider whose servant he is and what court he represents. A clerical jester is sadly out of place both in the pulpit and out of it. There should be a difference between a cheap advertising medium for a circus and an ambassador from the court of Heaven. It is to be feared that a preacher may grieve the Holy Spirit more by foolish talking and jesting than by anything else. If his strength has departed from him and he does not know the reason why, let him examine himself with this thought in mind.

IV. HE MUST TAKE CARE OF HIS BODILY HEALTH

Ordinarily a man must be a good animal before he can be a good preacher. The preacher should be in his best condition physically. A good physique is an attraction in the pulpit as well as the basis for good spiritual enjoyment. Spirituality and dyspepsia are very seldom found in the same individual at the same time. Let him exercise, take care of his health, look well to his diet. There are many spiritual enemies that cannot be cast out except "by prayer and fasting." A change of diet is the first thing some Christians need to attend to in order to progress in sanctification. The Apostle Paul also says, "Bodily exercise is profitable"; therefore, exercise.

Chapter 3

CHOICE OF THE TEXT

I. DEFINITION AND LENGTH

THE WORD "text" is from the Latin *textus* or *textum* and signifies something woven or spun. It is, therefore, that out of which the sermon is woven, the basis of the sermon or message. The text is not to be a mere motto for a sermon, nor is it to be chosen after the theme or subject is chosen and the sermon finished. If the sermon is not to be woven from the text, then the preacher must not take a text or pretend to do so. If he chooses a text, let it be a text and not a *pretext*. Sometimes texts are too apt to be "points of departure" for a sermon.

Whether texts should be long or short depends upon circumstances and usage. We are told that the early Christians chose long texts. From the seventeenth to the nineteenth centuries short texts were popular. Today the tendency seems to be toward the choice of long texts. The popular preaching is expository preaching.

II. THE CHOICE OF A TEXT

The importance of the right choice of the text upon which the sermon is based should not be underestimated. A young preacher, on asking what text he should choose for a sermon, was answered, "Oh, any text will do; speak on the Medes, Persians, Elamites, and the dwellers in Mesopotamia." This was certainly fatal advice to give to any young preacher.

The choice of a right text is often a difficult task for the preacher. No one knows better than he how nerve-wracking it is to have Saturday come and not to have found a text for the coming Sunday sermon. And often when a text is chosen under such conditions it is more of a pretext than a text.

Roman Catholic, Lutheran, and Episcopalian preachers have a great advantage over preachers of other denominations in that their texts have already been chosen for them by the Church. Because of the *Pericopes*, and Gospel and Epistle lessons for the year as found in the prayer books of these churches, they are saved the trouble of searching for texts. The Scripture lessons and the texts for the sermons are already mapped out for them. It may be that this is a good thing for the preacher, and it doubtless has many commendable qualities. If considered an ironclad rule, it may at times seem arbitrary and binding and cause a man to preach on a subject with which, for the time being at least, he is not in sympathy. Yet, on the other hand, it settles the mind and allows the preacher to quietly and calmly gather material for his sermon all the time. He is thus saved many a sleepless night.

III. THE ADVANTAGES OF HAVING A TEXT

There certainly are many important advantages accruing from having an aptly chosen text. Textless preachers are great losers in the matter of effective preaching.

A. It Awakens the Interest of the Audience

This is by no means an advantage to be ignored. To pass it by is fatal to the preacher. How many times, we have listened to a preacher announce his text, and our attention has been aroused by the very reading of it, have we said within ourselves, "I wonder what the preacher is going to get out of that text?" Thus at the outset our interest and attention has been secured. To be able to secure this state of mind in the audience is of great advantage to the preacher. He can well afford to give diligent attention to whatever will produce this result.

B. It Gains the Confidence of the Audience

Confidence—in that he is to proclaim to the people the Word of God and not his own opinions. The Word of God is to many people—it should be to everyone—an end to all controversy.

C. It Gives the Preacher Authority and Boldness in the Proclamation of His Message

He need speak in no vacillating or uncertain tone. With a "Thus saith the Lord" as the basis of his sermon, he may speak with the authority of Heaven, for, after all, it is God and not man who speaks from the text. With such an authoritative message no preacher need be timid about proclaiming the will of God. A timid preacher is a caricature and useless in the pulpit. To be sure one has a direct message from God gives the messenger a sense of authority and holy boldness.

D. It Will Keep the Preacher's Mind from Wandering

As anyone well knows, this is something to be greatly desired. Some preachers are like boys swimming under water. You see them when they dive off the text, and then you see them when they bob up again at the "Amen." But all through the sermon you lose sight of them because they have gone in over their heads. The text is a good thing with which to round a man up and bring him back from his wanderings. It constantly arouses the query, "Am I keeping to my text?"

E. It Will Keep the Preacher Biblical

This is a valuable thing in itself. There is not very much danger of running away from the Scriptures if he sticks closely to the exposition of the text. If ever there was a time when Biblical preachers are needed, it is now.

IV. THE GENERAL PRINCIPLES WHICH GOVERN THE CHOICE OF A TEXT

Phillips Brooks well said: "The ease and facility with which a text is chosen depends upon two things: the preacher's own mind, and the idea of a sermon." If the preacher's own mind is barren and sterile; if it is not fertile by being rooted in the Word of God; if the mind is dry and unspiritual because of not bathing the heart in the laver of the Word; then the choosing of a text will be a difficult task. But on the contrary: if the mind and soul of the preacher are being continually steeped in the Word of truth; if there is a daily walk and fellowship with God; then it will be a comparatively easy matter to find a text from which to proclaim God's message to a hungry world. Then again, if the minister has the idea that a sermon is a stilted affair, a great oration, an extraordinary deliverance, instead of a message from God through the life of the preacher to the hearts of men—a message straight from the preacher's heart to the hearer's soul—then it will indeed be a difficult task to choose the proper text.

And what is a great sermon after all? We often hear it said—probably because of such stilted ideas as to the nature of a sermon— that it is hard for any pastor to preach two *strong* sermons each Sunday. What is a great or a strong sermon? Certainly a sermon that accomplishes the desired result is a strong sermon. That a man cannot preach two such sermons each Sunday is born of a wrong conception as to what a sermon should be. Sermons ought to be messages straight from the heart of the preacher to the soul of the hearer. The people to whom a pastor ministers expect him to have been in communion and fellowship with God all through the week in a sense in which it has not been possible for them to be and that his messages on Sunday are to be to them the expression of what he has gathered from such communion and fellowship with his Lord. Is it not strange that after a week of such fellowship a man should be able to deliver only a weak sermon on Sunday evening?

A. One Must Carefully Consider the Spiritual Needs of the People to Whom One is Ministering

The preacher should study his people. He must consider their needs—physical, mental, moral, spiritual. He should ask himself what he has found out about their needs as the result of his visitation among them. Let him imagine his people gathered around his desk as he considers what to preach about, and let their needs determine what shall be the nature of his text and sermon. The preacher who is thus led will not fail to preach helpful sermons. He will often have his people say to him, "Pastor, your sermon has helped me, and I want to thank you for it."

B. There Should Be a Careful Consideration of the Cycle of Truth Preached

He must ask himself, "On what themes have I been preaching lately? Have I omitted any of the great doctrines of the Scriptures? Has my preaching been symmetrical, and has it included the whole counsel of God?" The choice of a text and a subject is not something that can be left to chance or to the whim of the preacher. The entire cycle of what he has preached upon before must be considered. For this reason it is a good thing for the preacher to draw up at the beginning of the year a list of the subjects upon which he intends to preach during that year.

The Episcopal and Lutheran churches, in arranging the Gospel lessons which form the texts from which their ministers preach, divide the church year into two great parts: justification—what Christ has done *for* us; sanctification—what Christ does *in* us. Thus, beginning with the advent and concluding with the second coming of Christ, the whole cycle of truth is covered. Is there not a lesson for preachers of other denominations to learn from this arrangement? They shall thus at least be saved from being faddists or hobbyists in their preaching.

C. There Should Be a Careful Consideration of One's Ability to Deal with the Text and the Subject Derived from It

It is not well for David to go to battle in Saul's armor. A preacher must not choose subjects that are above and beyond his ability to handle. Little ships must keep near to the shore or they will be wrecked. This does not mean he must never handle subjects that are in advance of his present educational attainments, for then there would be no growth in his experience or preaching. It does mean, however, that before he preaches on a subject he must understand clearly for himself whatever phase of it he may present. It is well for the young preacher to avoid controversial themes.

He should remember these three general principles when choosing a text; the spiritual needs of the people; the cycle of truth preached; and his own ability to present the subject.

V. THE PARTICULAR PRINCIPLES WHICH GOVERN THE CHOICE OF A TEXT

A. The Constant Reading of the Word of God Is Primary

Let the messenger of God study his Bible; it is the great quarry of the preacher. The Bible is not merely a textbook; it is a book of texts. Therefore, the Scriptures should be read constantly. "It [the Bible] contains the truths we have to teach, the laws which we have to illustrate in their relations to the lives of our people, the divine promises by which we are to console them when in trouble and to strengthen their faith in the love and power of God."— DALE

B. The Use of a Notebook Should Be Cultivated

Let him read with a notebook at his hand. Whenever any thought, illustration, or argument impresses him, he should make a note of it. An hour's reading will often furnish suggestive material for two or three sermons. Again, he will find in his reading of the Scriptures that a certain text will impress itself upon his mind very vividly. Indeed, an outline of the theme suggested by the text may loom up before him. If so, he should write down the text and the thoughts that have thus associated themselves with it.

Some day when it is difficult to find a text, one need only turn to the notebook and find one there already suggestively outlined. He should jot down important thoughts as they come to him, making a note not merely of the reference to the page or location, but working out the headings with the thoughts that suggest themselves to him at the time. The outline should be worked out there and then. At some future time when he feels barren, he may draw on this fresh manna. In this way he will have a constant supply of raw material. The preachers who form and keep up this habit are never at a loss for material.

C. The Reading of Good Books Provides Rich Sermon Material

They should be read not to copy and adopt, but to inspire and adapt. They can be a tonic for the mind. Reading good books acts as water poured down a dry pump—it primes and has a reactionary effect. The lives of great preachers, missionaries, reformers, and so on should be absorbed. The study of biography is a great inspiration to the preacher.

D. The Guidance of the Holy Spirit Is Paramount

The preacher should seek the Spirit's guidance. Spurgeon said, "You can say truly what Jacob said falsely, 'The Lord hath brought it to me.' While other men, as Esau, may be hunting for their sermon material or texts in the distant places, you, by the help of the Spirit may find the savory morsel right close to home." The man who is continually living under the influence and power of the Holy Spirit will scarcely ever be at a loss for something to preach about.

VI. CERTAIN PRECAUTIONS NECESSARY IN THE CHOICE OF TEXTS

A. Let the Preacher Be Warned against the Choosing of Odd Texts

A few illustrations will explain what is meant. A minister preached a sermon to a number of tailors and took for his text: "A remnant shall be saved." Another, addressing an audience of newspaper reporters, took for his text the words: "And he sought to see Jesus who he was; and could not for the press." An English minister, addressing a bench of English judges, based his remarks on the text: "Judge not, and ye shall not be judged." A young Episcopal clergyman made himself ridiculous in the eyes of his congregation by preaching on a certain Ash Wednesday from the text: "I have eaten ashes like bread." Other illustrations are the following: "Take it by the tail" (Exodus 4:4); "I have put off my coat, how shall I put it on?"

A sermon aimed against women coiling their hair on the top of their heads had as its text the words: "Top [k]not come down," a gross violation of both the grammar and sense of the Scripture as found in Matthew 24: "Let him which is on the housetop not come down." It is recorded that a minister preached eleven sermons on the letter "O."

"Such texts may please the idle-minded and vain, but will distress all who come to worship God and receive His message at the preacher's lips. Have you any particular sermons on striking texts? Take a friend's advice and burn them."—Joseph Parker

"When I hear a man announce a text of this sort and watch the process by which he develops from it the doctrine of justification by faith, or the necessity of regeneration, or a theory of divine providence, or some interesting

speculations on the millennium or the future blessedness
of the righteous, I always think of the tricks of those ingenious gentlemen who entertain the public by rubbing a
sovereign between their hands until it becomes a canary,
and drawing out of their coat sleeves half a dozen brilliant
glass globes filled with water, and with four or five gold
fish swimming in each of them. For myself I like to listen
to a good preacher, and I have no objection in the world to
be amused by the tricks of a clever conjurer; but I prefer to
keep the conjuring and the preaching separate: conjuring
on Sunday morning, conjuring in the church, conjuring
with texts of Scripture, is not quite to my taste. When the
text is only a deceptive signal, or when a steeple surmounts
a play house, it would doubtless be better to remove the
signal and throw down the steeple."—DALE

B. He Must Not Choose a Text Which, Because of Surrounding Circumstances, Will Appear Ridiculous

The feature of such blunders which is especially bad is
that associations clinging to a passage of Scripture may be
of such a character that its repetition shall ever after occasion a smile, even in the house of God. For this reason
we hesitate to give the reader the following illustrations
and give them only to leave a deeper impression touching
the dangers to which preachers are unfortunately exposed.

On the first visit after his marriage to the home of his
bride, a minister surprised and convulsed the congregation
with laughter by announcing for his text, "Oh, that I were
as in months past." A preacher of ponderous physical pro-
portions, with a corresponding ponderous manuscript
which he placed on the desk after having piled thereon
two Bibles and several hymnbooks, rose to his full height,

took a long breath, and read for his text the words, "Thou shalt see greater things than these." An extremely corpulent clergyman announced for his text, "If any man thinketh that he hath whereof he might trust in the flesh, I more."

C. He Must Not Choose Texts That Create Expectations Which Neither the Sermon Nor the Preacher Can Fulfill

For instance, young preachers should hesitate before preaching on such themes as: "The glory of Heaven"; "And there was a rainbow round about the throne"; "We all do fade as a leaf"; "And the streets of the city were of pure gold." Since "Eye hath not seen, nor ear heard," what is the use of trying to picture it? But what shall the preacher do with such texts? Shall he ignore them altogether? By no means. Let him take a more simple text and weave these grand thoughts into the sermon.

D. He Must Not Choose Questionable Texts

John 9:31 furnishes a good example: "We know that God heareth not sinners." These words of the blind man can hardly be true, for God does hear sinners—for instance, the publican in the temple.

Let him exercise care with reference to the choosing of texts from the books of Job and Ecclesiastes. The purpose of the book, the character of the spokesman, and the comparison of scripture with scripture should be taken into consideration.

E. Let Him Not Use Mutilated Texts

It is neither wise nor right to use as texts for sermons such passages as only partly express the mind and sense of the writer, for instance, "All men are liars"; "There is no God"; "John the Baptist is risen from the dead." A half-truth is worse than a lie.

"Satan's first lie was a half truth. He told our first parents that to eat the forbidden fruit would open their eyes, and it did, but it was to see themselves sinners; he said they would know both good and evil, and so they did; but how much better it would have been to know only good! He said they should not, in the day they ate, surely die; and they did not, in the low sense of physical death, though they did die to God's favor and sympathy. Satan's favorite device for deluding and destroying souls is to use half truths."—A. T. PIERSON

Let preachers beware lest they fall into this snare of the devil.

F. Old Testament Texts Should Not Be Neglected

The Old Testament as well as the New is the inspired Word of God. "All Scripture . . . is profitable" for the preacher to choose his texts from. The Old Testament as well as the New instructs in righteousness and should therefore not be neglected, even though the New Testament may yield the richer sermonic treasures.

Chapter 4

INTERPRETATION OF THE TEXT

I. RULES FOR THE INTERPRETATION OF A TEXT*

THERE MUST be due recognition of the rules that determine the meaning of the text which is to form the basis of a sermon. The rules are as follows:

A. The Preacher Should Ascertain Whether the Language of the Text Is Literal or Figurative

Usually the Bible interprets its own terms and by means of the context informs the reader whether the language used is to be taken in a literal sense. This cannot be accomplished by intellectual science alone. Judgment, good faith, critical tact, and impartiality are also necessary. It is necessary to examine the passage in all its details, critically, exegetically, and faithfully. The figurative sense must be sustained by all these processes before it can be relied upon as the true interpretation.

Our Saviour spoke in figurative language when He said to the Jews: "Destroy this temple, and in three days I will raise it up." How do we know this language is figurative? In this instance the narrator says so (John 2:19, 21-22).

So it is with Matthew 26:26-27; Mark 14:22-24; Luke

*See William Evans, *The Book of Books.*

22:19-20; I Corinthians 11:23-26, in which reference is made to the elements used in the celebration of the Eucharist. It is not literally Jesus' flesh and blood which are spoken of in these passages, but His flesh and blood represented under the figure of bread and wine.

The words "washing" and "wash" are often used figuratively as well as literally in the Bible. When Naaman was told to "wash in Jordan seven times," it is impossible not to see that the word is to be taken in its literal sense. But when, as in I Corinthians 6:11, believing Christians are spoken of as being "washed," it is equally manifest that the word is used figuratively, and that they are washed in the sense of being cleansed from their sin and released from its consequences by the saving efficacy of the blood of Christ.

The literal language of Scripture is to be preferred unless otherwise demanded by the context, parallel passages, or analogy. The simple rules of grammar should be applied as directed by a wide-awake common sense, taking for granted the Bible means just what it says. True, we are warned that the letter killeth, and the spirit giveth life; but we are also told that every jot and tittle of the law is to be fulfilled. It is better to be unyieldingly literal than to adopt rationalistic interpretations of the Gospel that make the Word of God of none effect. But we need the twofold caution: neither to add to nor to take from, especially not to put into the Bible a doctrine that is not there. To find out just what the Bible says will require close study.

B. He Must Ascertain the Meaning of Words as Used by Each Writer of the Scriptures

All the writers do not give the same word exactly the same meaning. The usage of the writer and the connection in which it is used must determine the meaning of the particular word.

The word "faith" is an example. In Galatians 1:23; I Timothy 3:9; 4:1; Acts 24:24 it means the Gospel of which faith in Christ is the great doctrine. In Romans 3:3 it means truth or faithfulness—the fidelity of God in keeping His word. In Acts 17:31 the Greek word which is elsewhere usually translated "faith" but here "assurance," means proof or evidence. In Romans 14:23 it means a conscientious conviction of duty.

Again, one can take the word "flesh." In Ezekiel 11:19 it is used in contrast to stone. In John 1:14; Romans 1:3; 9:3 it refers to human nature without any reference to sinfulness. In Romans 8:13 and Ephesians 2:3 it points to human nature as both sinful and corrupt.

So it is with the word "salvation." In Exodus 14:13 it means outward safety and deliverance; in James 5:15 bodily healing ("will save"); in Romans 13:11 the whole of the blessing which Christ has secured for believers. Sometimes it means simply the Gospel, as in Hebrews 2:3.

1. Sometimes the Sense in Which the Word is Used Is Made Known or Defined by the Writer Himself.

In Hebrews 11, for instance, "faith" is first defined and then illustrated. It is said to be a confident expectation of things hoped for, a perfect persuasion of things not seen; and then examples are given of both parts of this definition.

The word "perfection"—over which so many are stumbling in this day—is clearly defined in the several parts of the Bible. In Psalm 37:37 it is used as being synonymous with uprightness or sincerity, a real, unfeigned goodness in opposition to sham goodness; and this is doubtless its real meaning in the Old Testament (I Chron. 12:33, 38). In the New Testament the word "perfect" means either the possession of clear and accurate knowledge of divine truth, or the possession of *all* the graces of Christian character in a higher or lower degree. The first is the meaning in Hebrews 5:14 (A.V., "of full age"); I Corinthians 2:6; Philippians 3:15. The second is the meaning in James 1:4; A.S.V., where the word is defined as "entire, lacking in nothing." In II Peter 1:5-7 the graces which characterize the perfect Christian are enumerated.

2. SOMETIMES WORDS ARE TO BE UNDERSTOOD, ACCORDING TO THE CONTEXT, TO MEAN THE VERY OPPOSITE OF THEIR USUAL SENSE.

In I Kings 22:15, "Go, and prosper" was spoken ironically and meant the very reverse.

In Numbers 22:20, "Rise up, and go" appears from verses 12 and 32 to mean, "If your heart is set on violating My command after all I have told you, then do it at your own risk."

The use of this form of speech may also be seen in I Kings 18:27; Judges 10:14; Mark 7:9; I Corinthians 4:8.

C. He Must Consider the Circumstances Peculiar to the Writer and Those Written to

We should be more likely to translate literally what we find in the historical books than what we find in the poetical books. We should be more likely to emphasize chronology than the details of parables.

The student of the Scriptures must become well acquainted with the individuality of each writer, his style, and mode of expression.

Under what circumstances were the words written, what

was the character of the people to whom they were addressed, and what state of moral sentiment prevailed at the time of writing? One must take cognizance of these and other circumstances peculiar to each book and author if he would become a true and safe interpreter of the Bible.

D. He Must Compare Scripture with Scripture (Rom. 12:6)

The more one studies the Word of God, the more one recognizes a divine unity running through the Scriptures which is a proof of its inspiration. The phrase "the whole tenor of Scripture" means a gathering together of all the passages bearing upon any one subject and comparing them the one with the other, thereby arriving at the teaching of "the whole Scripture" on that given subject. For example, if an expositor were to speak of justification by faith as though it freed us from obligation to holiness, such an interpretation must be rejected, because it contradicts the main design and spirit of the Gospel.

In Proverbs 16:4 it is said, "The Lord hath made all things for himself: yea, even the wicked for the day of evil." The doctrine that the wicked were created that they might be condemned, which some have founded upon this passage, is inconsistent with innumerable parts of Scripture and therefore cannot be true (Ps. 145:9; Ezek. 18:23; II Peter 3:9). The meaning, as determined by the comparison of scripture with scripture, is that all evil shall contribute to the glory of God and promote the accomplishment of His adorable designs.

"The Scriptures being composed of several obscure texts of Scripture mingled with clear ones, many devout persons have rather chosen to read other books, which, being free from difficulties, might promise more instruction; but as

the moon, notwithstanding her spots, gives more light than
the stars that are luminous, so the Scripture, notwithstanding its dark passages, will afford a Christian more light
than the best authors."—BOYLE (1627-1691)

"Make the Word of God as much as possible its own interpreter. You will best understand the Word of God by
comparing it with itself, 'comparing spiritual things with
spiritual.'"—BISHOP NEWTON

Thus we see that devout Christian men of all ages have
been impressed with the necessity of reading the Word of
God reverently and comparing scripture with scripture.

E. He Should Seek to Know the Manners and Customs of the People to Whom the Bible Was Originally Written

The houses of the poor in the East were generally made
of mud and thus become fitting images of the frailty of
human life. This fact helps us to understand such passages
as Job 24:16; Ezekiel 12:5, and Matthew 6:19.

The houses of the rich were of a more elaborate order,
comprising porches, porticoes, waiting rooms, guestcham-
bers. The roof was flat, surrounded by a battlement of
breastwork. In summer the people slept on the roof, and
at all times it was used as a place of prayer and devotion.
These facts explain the following and many other passages: Deuteronomy 22:8; I Samuel 9:25; II Samuel 11:2;
Isaiah 22:1; Mark 2:4; 13:15; and Acts 10:9.

The dress of the Jews consisted commonly of two garments: the one a close-bodied frock or shirt, generally
with long sleeves, reaching a little below the knee, and
later to the ankle; the other a loose robe of some yards in
length, fastened over the shoulders and thrown around
the body. Within doors the first dress only was worn.

However, it was regarded as a kind of undress, in which it was not usual to pay visits or to walk out. Therefore persons clothed in it alone are said in Scripture to be naked (Isa. 20:2-4; John 13:4 and 21:7) or to have laid aside their garments.

II. THE SOURCES OF THE INTERPRETATION OF THE TEXT

The sources of interpretation are four: the text, the context, parallel passages, and resources outside of the text. It is absolutely necessary that these be taken into consideration by the student. In no other way can a correct exegesis of any portion of the sacred writings be obtained.

A. The Preacher Must Study the Text Itself

The first thing to be done in the study of any text is to find out what the text itself really teaches.

In this connection a knowledge of the *original languages* of the Bible is found exceedingly valuable. It affords the student an opportunity of ascertaining the various shades of meaning which are impossible to find in a translation. If he can, then, he should study the text in the language in which it was originally written. Let him find out the exact meaning of each word, phrase, and sentence. Let there be no hurry or haste in the matter. The preacher owes such diligent and thorough study of the text to God, to the Scriptures, to himself, and to the people to whom he ministers.

The student who is not able to read the text in the original need not despair of being able to ascertain its true meaning, for the American Standard Version comes to his help. In spite of its inconsistencies this version is beyond question a very good translation. Study the text in the American Standard as well as in the Authorized Version. A comparison of I Thessalonians 4:15 in the Authorized and American Standard versions will illustrate the advantage of the latter. The word "prevent" in the Authorized is correctly translated "precede" in the American Standard Version. The word originally meant "to go before," but words sometimes become obsolete or change their meaning. Here is an illustration of the latter.

In his search for truth he should not be on the lookout for the brilliant and ingenious, but for the true. Nor should he sacrifice truth for brilliancy or for the sake of making an impression. He must not juggle with the Scriptures. In all things it behooves students and teachers to rightly divide the Word of truth.

One ought to also remember in this connection that invaluable help in the study of the text is to be found in the similarity between the Old and New Testament language of the same text. One can compare Psalm 8:3-8 with Hebrews 2:5-8.

For helps to the study of the *text itself*, one could make use of concordances, such as *Young's Analytical Concordance* and *Strong's Exhaustive Concordance*, and of commentaries, such as *Jamieson, Fausset, and Brown; Keil and Delitzsch; Alford's Greek Testament;* and *The Wycliffe Bible Commentary.*

B. He Should Note the Context

The context is what goes before and what follows after the special portion of the sacred text under consideration.

To find the real context of a passage one may have to go back one or more chapters. An illustration is chapter 7 of Romans. Before this chapter can be correctly interpreted it is necessary to go back to chapter 1 and grasp the thought of the whole book.

Another passage worth noticing is II Timothy 3:16. This verse is constantly quoted as a proof text for the inspiration of the whole Bible. It concerns the Old Testament only, as the New Testament was not as yet written. It does announce the great truth that the Old Testament is inspired of God. One must look to other sources for proof of the inspiration of the New Testament.

Many interpreters neglect the context. They snatch a word out of its connection and thus get a distorted view of scriptural teaching. Some time ago a sermon was preached on Hebrews 7:25. The preacher in a very brilliant manner sought to show the power of Christ to save the lowest and most degraded of sinners. Especially did he emphasize the word "uttermost" to prove the power of Christ. Now, this text does not prove Christ's ability to save sinners of the worst kind, although many other passages do (for instance, I Tim. 1:15; Luke 19:10; Isa. 1:18). Had the preacher read the context carefully he would not have chosen this passage as the text for such a theme. The context shows that this passage sets forth the difference between the priesthood of Christ and that of the Levites: they, by reason of death, could minister only temporarily; He, by reason of His ever living, is able to save (or minister) *for evermore*. The word "uttermost" is best translated "completely." The context demands such a translation (see A.S.V., margin).

The preacher must study the context, reading carefully what *goes before* and what *comes after* the passage he is seeking to expound. See also Matthew 5:48 (p. 67) and Hebrews 6:1.

C. He Should Make Use of Parallel Passages

Obscure words and phrases will thus become clear and plain.

"Particular diligence should be used in comparing the parallel texts of the Old and New Testaments. It should be a rule with everyone who would read the Holy Scriptures with advantage and improvement, to compare every text which may seem either important for the doctrine it may contain or remarkable for the turn of expression with the parallel passages in other parts of Holy Writ, that is, with passages in which the subject matter is the same, the sense equivalent, or the turn of expression similar."
—Horsley

God, for example, sometimes represents Himself as giving men to drink of a cup which He holds in His hand; they take it and fall prostrate to the ground in fearful intoxication. The figure is given with much brevity and with no word of explanation in some of the prophecies (Nahum 3:11; Hab. 2:16; Ps. 75:8). In Isaiah 51:17-23 it is fully explained, and the meaning of the figure becomes clear.

In Mark 8:36 we have the words: "For what shall it profit a man, if he shall gain the whole world, and lose his own soul?" What is meant here by the word "soul"? The study of the parallel passage in Luke 9:25 throws light on the word. It reads as follows: "For what is a man advantaged, if he gain the whole world, and lose *himself*?" From these two passages we learn that "soul" and "himself" are equivalent.

D. He Can Use Resources outside the Text

After the student has carefully and prayerfully studied the text, the context, and the parallel passages, he may safely read what other authorities have to say on the text. Cogitation first, the thoughts of others afterward.

The resources outside the text include commentaries, concordances, text expositions, word and subject indexes and other library helps.

Chapter 5

THEME

THE WISE CHOICE and proper wording of the theme of a sermon are matters of no small importance. The attractiveness of the title of a book is sometimes the greatest factor in its sale. While this should not be so in the case of a sermon, yet it must be admitted that a wisely chosen theme has much to do with the sermon's interest to its hearers.

A few general suggestions bearing on the subject are given here:

I. THE PREACHER SHOULD KNOW HIS THEME THOROUGHLY

This does not mean the preacher must know absolutely everything connected with the subject. However, it does mean he must have a clear, definite, intelligent, masterly grasp of the subject. He might become familiar with the theme by talking the subject over with someone. If one cannot express the theme colloquially, it is doubtful if he can do so from the pulpit.

It may be said in this connection that it is by no means always wise to preach at once upon a theme because one is deeply impressed with it at the time. One will preach better if he allows the matter to revolve more and more in his mind. Let him live in the theme; let it be the atmos-

phere which he breathes, let it master and take complete
possession of him—*then* let him preach about it. Knowledge is power in this as well as in all other respects. From
this it may be said he should preach on familiar themes,
at least to begin with. This is good advice to young
preachers. The older ones do not need it, for they know
it from experience, and often bitter-experience at that.

II. LET HIM BE SURE HIS THEME IS ONE HIS HEARERS CAN READILY UNDERSTAND

He must not preach over people's heads. The preacher
should remember that his hearers do not live in the same
kind of atmosphere he does throughout the week. What is
very commonplace to him may be quite strange to them.
Hence it is not prudent to discuss from the pulpit the au-
thorship of the Pentateuch or whether one or two authors
wrote Isaiah. The average audience is not at all interested
in the discussion of such questions. The people are soul-
hungry; they want bread and not stones.

How disinterested the average audience is in such
themes may be seen by watching their faces. How bored
they look when such abstract subjects are discussed! How
bright and interested when the appeal is made to something that will help them in their everyday life!

It is not intended by these remarks that one must never
preach on a theme unless the audience is familiar with it.
The preacher is an educator, and as such there are times
when he will find it necessary to deal with a theme which
may be new and strange to the hearers. But even in such
cases let the arguments, illustrations, and analogies be such
that the congregation may reasonably be expected to understand.

III. HE DARE NOT LET HIS THEME BE A
TRIVIAL ONE

Usually one has only two sermons a week to preach;
therefore, let him choose a theme that has weight and
dignity. Reading the headlines in the daily papers will
teach a lesson in this direction. Sermons have been
preached on such themes as "The Crown of Thorns," "The
Folded Napkin," "The Rainbow about the Throne," details
which no doubt are interesting in themselves, but which
are not in themselves big enough to constitute a sermon.
These things make nice scenery, but very small subjects.
It would be better to preach about the Christ who wore
the crown of thorns; the resurrection, of which the folded
napkin was but an incident; the Judge who sits upon the
throne. The sculptors of Greece, famous in history, did
not spend their time carving cherry stones; they carved
Minervas, Apollos, and Jupiters. Let the preacher speak
on the great doctrines, the fundamentals, the stupendous
truths of the Bible and our redemption. As someone has
said, it is not necessary to expend consecrated energy in
striking gnats with a club of Hercules.

IV. HE SHOULD HAVE A DEFINITE AIM IN
THE TREATMENT OF HIS THEME

He does not dare go into the pulpit simply because it
is Sunday and he is expected to deliver a message. It is not
so much the question of preaching something as preaching
with a definite end and aim in view. He must preach so
that if anyone were to stop him in the midst of his sermon
and ask him what he was aiming at, he could give a definite answer. He must aim to hit something, not rambling
here and there. He should have a mark; aim at it; hit it;
stop and see where the shot struck; then fire another

shot straight from the shoulder. Letters not addressed or wrongly addressed are sent to the dead-letter office; they are of no use to anybody. Preaching for conversions and decisions is needed. There is too much generalized preaching today—in fact, there always has been since apostolic times. A young preacher once expressed his sorrow to Mr. Spurgeon that there had been so few conversions under his preaching. "Why," said Mr. Spurgeon, "you don't expect conversions to follow every sermon, do you?" "Oh, no, of course not," the young man replied. "Then you certainly won't have them," responded Mr. Spurgeon. One minister remarked to another concerning a newly settled metropolitan pastor, "They say he actually expects conversions at the morning service!" What would happen to the Church of Christ if every evangelist and pastor were to "expect conversions in the morning," and preach with that end in view? Paul's idea of preaching was to persuade men to be reconciled to God. That seems to be a desirable end today. Let us have less firing of blank cartridges and more shooting to kill.

V. HE DOES NOT DARE CHOOSE A THEME THAT HE EITHER DOES NOT LIKE OR HAS NOT EXPERIENCED

This does not mean one shall never preach on a theme of which he has not yet reached the fullness in his own experience. There will always be illimitable stretches in Christian experience of which we must say, "I have not yet attained," but which "I follow after." Nevertheless there are certain phases of Christian life and character, even above that attained by the average Christian, which a congregation has a right to expect from its minister.

He had better not preach holiness if he is not living a

holy life. If he is constantly sad, he cannot preach on
the joy of the Lord. Let him first be joyful, then preach
about it. He cannot proclaim in loud pulpit tones the
blessedness of a life of victory over sin if he is not enjoying
a victorious life himself. "Physician, heal thyself." No
preacher can afford to falsely impersonate. An actor may
play a role, but a preacher must not.

The results of such inconsistent, unsympathetic preaching will be a hardening of the preacher's heart, a blunting
of his perceptions, and the cultivating of a general tone of
insincerity. Let him hear the words of the Apostle: "Thou
that preachest a man should not steal, dost thou steal?
Thou that makest thy boast of the law, through breaking
the law dishonorest thou God?"

VI. HE SHOULD LET HIS THEME BE SUITABLE TO TIME, PLACE, AND OCCASION

If it is Easter, one should preach on the resurrection of
Christ; if Christmas, on the birth of Christ; if Passion
Week, on the death of Christ. In so doing he is able to
take advantage of the sentiment already existing in the
minds of his people in favor of his theme. Ordinarily the
preacher has to pour floods upon the dry ground of the
minds of his hearers before the seed of truth can find lodg-
ment, but during these festival seasons the ground for the
reception of the truth has already been prepared to a very
great extent.

This conception is true also with reference to the adaptation of the truth to the various kinds of congregations
to whom one may be called to minister. The truth itself
does not need to be changed, merely the adaptation of it
to the particular congregation. The late Dr. John Hall
of New York is reported to have once said before a gradu-

ating class of theological students that he preached precisely the same Gospel truth to his rich and cultured congregation on Fifth Avenue as he did to his first charge in
a rural district. Of course he presented the same truth in
a form which his changed audiences could appreciate. He
adopted the same truth, but adapted it to the varying conditions. The Apostle Paul presented the same truth to
different auditors in different ways. For example, when
speaking to the Athenian philosophers, he referred to their
"poets," while in speaking to a rural audience he spoke
of the "fruitful harvests" God had sent them.

Chapter 6

GATHERING SERMON
MATERIAL

IT IS ASSUMED the text and theme of the sermon have already been decided upon. Now comes the time for asking questions. This implies reflection. The preacher should reflect before beginning to write a single word of the sermon. And in reflecting one must value his own thought. He must: be himself; insist upon himself; be willing to be himself; and believe in the worth of his own reflection. No matter what it may cost by way of self-denial and self-sacrifice one must insist on thinking for himself. Let him present his own thoughts and reflections in his preaching, shine in his own star rather than in someone else's sun. He may lose some of the popularity he has falsely made, but inevitably and ultimately he will gain his own respect and that of his audience. Many a preacher knows well what it is to have a sermon pass over him but not go through him, to have it pass over his lips but not through his own brain and heart. Let him be himself, his best self, being willing to shine in his own light rather than in the light of others. "Thou shalt not steal" is a commandment that may be broken by the appropriation or the misappropriation of another man's sermon preached as though it were altogether one's own production.

Here are some questions that should be asked as one proceeds to prepare the sermon:

I. WHAT HAVE I EVER READ ON THIS SUBJECT?

As the preacher ponders this question, he should gather his thoughts together. Let him think, writing as he thinks, paying no attention to the order in which the thoughts come into the mind. Thought is of primary importance now; the order of the thought, secondary.

Some people do not have many thoughts on the particular subject because they are not readers. To be prolific in thought one must be a faithful reader. Reading makes a wise man. The constant reader will not be at a loss for thoughts. The man who does not read much will not make much of a preacher. One good sermon a day and one good book a week ought to be the minimum intellectual diet of every man who would be a good preacher. Not to read is to have nothing to draw from except oneself, and often one feels himself to be a dry subject indeed. Reading is a tonic; it has a reactionary effect upon the mind.

What should a man read? History, science, biography, books of scientific illustration, the daily papers, and magazines are all good reading; even good fiction is not to be lightly cast aside. But above all else in importance is the reading of the Bible. The reading of the Bible should not be spasmodic, but systematic and regular. Reading the Bible simply for the sake of getting a text from it and then closing it to resort to books of sermons for material is a practice that must end disastrously for the preacher. One must never neglect the study of the Bible on any account. Also, let the preacher read good books, cherishing the companionship of great minds. He must not neglect what God has said to the race through the minds and words of good and great men. He is a great scholar indeed who thinks he can afford to dispense with reading what others have written.

II. WHAT HAVE I OBSERVED THAT WILL THROW LIGHT ON THIS SUBJECT?

The preacher needs to have wide-open eyes. To have eyes and yet not see, ears and yet not hear, is fatal to the preacher. There are men who can never see "sermons in stones and books in running brooks" because they are used to seeing sermons in books and stones in running brooks. Said the prophet of the olden days concerning the dry and uninteresting preachers of his day: "They have seen nothing, they have no vision, and my people are perishing for the lack of preachers who have wide-open eyes and ears."

What is the difference between the man standing there in the meadow and the cow feeding by his side? In the one instance the cow has eyes and ears, but sees nothing except the grass it is eating and hears nothing but the inarticulate bellowing of the other cattle. Whereas, the man lifts up his eyes and sees afar off the beautiful hills and the enchanting landscape and listens to and appreciates the babbling of the little brook that runs at his feet. Man has been endowed by the Creator with eyes to see, ears to hear, and a mind to appreciate the beauty and utility of that which surrounds him.

Henry Ward Beecher stood one day in front of the window of a jewelry store in Brooklyn for about one hour, then went into the store and asked the proprietor—a personal friend—to allow him to have a few jewels to take home with him for a day or two. This permission was granted. On the following Sunday the great preacher announced as his text the words: "And they shall be mine, saith the

Lord of hosts, in that day when I make up my jewels."
Those who heard that sermon spoke of it as one of the best
ever heard from the pulpit of the Plymouth Church.
Beecher had eyes and saw things. Many a less observant
preacher would have seen and admired and gone his way,
and that would have been the end of his seeing.

How observant Christ was. His sermons abound with
illustrations taken from the things He saw and heard. For
example: "Behold a sower"; "Two women . . . grinding at
the mill"; "Consider the lilies"; "Have ye not heard?" and
so on. Jesus was all the time seeing and hearing things
and making use of them in His sermons.

The preacher should carry a notebook with him so he
can jot down the things he sees and hears that impress
him. Wherever he is and whatever he may be doing, let
him keep an open eye and ear for material to use in his
sermons. He will then have less need, if indeed any, of
resorting to stock illustration books. His matter will be
fresh and interesting.

An Irishman stood beholding the Niagara Falls for the
first time. An American stood by his side, entranced by
the greatness and grandeur of the mighty scene. "Is it not
a marvelous sight?" exclaimed the American. "Faith," said
the son of the Emerald Isle, "an' I see nothing to hinder
it." The Irishman had eyes and ears, but he neither saw
nor heard. An American woman, beholding the same wonder of nature, and being asked what she thought of it, replied, "Isn't it cute?" She also lacked the powers of observation. How different with the keen businessman, having the open eye and the open ear, who, when he looked
at those immense falls, cried, "Give me the use of those
falls, and I will light the city of Buffalo and run all its

machinery with its power." This man had eyes to see and
ears to hear.

When riding on the bus or the train, when driving, when
walking through the woods and fields, when sailing, when
participating in the social functions of life, or engaged in
the business of the day, the minister needs to keep his eyes
and ears open for material to illustrate truth. How many
people spend hours in the woods, surrounded by all the
beauty and glory of nature, and yet see nothing. The poet
speaks of such an one in these words:

> A primrose by a river's brim,
> A yellow primrose was to him
> And it was nothing more.

> One impulse from a vernal wood
>   May teach you more of man,
> Of moral evil, and of good,
>   Than all the sages can.

Therefore, as he sees things with his eyes and hears them
with his ears, these should be observed and recorded in a
notebook. At the close of each day he should ask himself,
"What have I learned from the things I have seen and
heard today?" He should not allow one day to pass without making some record, no matter how small, of something he has observed. If he is a keen observer, his sermons
will show it, and his audience will recognize and be
profited.

III. WHAT HAVE I EVER THOUGHT ON THIS SUBJECT?

Dr. A. T. Pierson speaks of what is called the principle
of "unconscious cerebration—a process which corresponds
to the incubation of an egg; the gradual and unconscious

formation of an idea in the mind. You have a thought
today; you make a record of it; you draw it out somewhat
in a memorandum and lay it aside. A month later you
take your memorandum. The thought has unconsciously
matured. You have been incubating your own conception,
and it is growing towards completeness though you have
been unconscious with regard to any mental process concerning it." So a man ought to be writing down thoughts
on various subjects as they come to him from time to time
and adding to them continually as they develop in his
mind. Many of our best thoughts have been lost because
we have failed to write them down. It is a good thing for
a man to write down at least one thought a day.

"It is a wise proverb among the learned, borrowed from
the lips and the practice of a celebrated painter, '*Nulla dies
sine linea,*' let no day pass without at least one line. It
was a sacred rule among the Pythagoreans, that they
should every evening run over the actions and affairs of
the day, and examine what their conduct had been, what
they had done, and what they had neglected; and they as-
sured their pupils, that by this method they would make
a noble progress in the path of virtue."—WATTS

IV. WHAT HAVE I GATHERED ON THIS SUBJECT?

A pitiable and deplorable sight is to see a minister a day
or two before the weekend fuming and fretting about his
sermon for the coming Sunday. Friday has come, and he
has hardly a single thought on the subject of his Sunday
sermon. He has now to begin to create all new material
for the sermon. It is nothing short of a disgrace for any
minister to have to create weekly all the material for each

sermon he prepares. It indicates he has not been in the habit of preserving the results of his reading, observation, and meditation. He has been treating his mind as a sieve— allowing every thought to pass through it. Or it may be he has overburdened his memory by committing to it tasks which in this day of filing devices are both unnecessary and impossible.

Not long ago a minister came into a fellow minister's study in a state of great perplexity. He moaned: "I have to deliver an address on Washington before a large assembly within a few days, and I regret to say I cannot lay my hand on any material for the address. I am sure I have material somewhere in my library on this theme, but just where I do not know. I am almost distracted; can you help me?" Here was a preacher who was supposed to be constantly reading, observing, meditating with eyes, ears, hands, pen and paper, yet had gathered nothing in all the years on such an important personage as George Washington. It was not that he had not read or heard many things in connection with this great historical character, for he had; the trouble was he had not preserved the results of years and put it away in such shape and manner as to lay hands on it whenever needed. It seems there is absolutely no excuse for this state of affairs. His colleague instructed him: "My friend, do you see that index filing cabinet yonder? Well, just stoop down, put your hand on the envelope marked 'Wa,' take it home with you, and you will find material enough there to make six addresses on Washington."

When we remember that a man's future success may depend upon one address and that he may be called upon to deliver that address after only a few hours' notice, does it not seem utter folly to neglect proper classification and filing away of the material he may gather each day from reading and observation?

The preacher must be gathering constantly. The danger of gathering only at the time of preparing the sermon is that the preacher will possess and the people will receive only half-digested thoughts. Many preachers, reading over sermons preached a few months or perhaps only a few weeks before, have found themselves remarking, "Well, did I say that? Did I really give expression to that thought? Did I really teach that truth? I did not know I ever preached that." The thoughts preached have gone over the lips of the preacher, but not through his heart and mind. They were not really his. Many a minister's sermons are scattered over with thoughts he possessed but for a moment. The good preacher will be gathering material for his sermons all the time and will daily file it away for future use.

After all, the preacher's main business is not to preach sermons; it is to gather and proclaim truth. Therefore the preacher's whole life should be spent in seeking for truth for truth's sake and not for the mere sake of sermon preparation. He must learn to gather his material before he undertakes the preparation of his sermon. During the process of building, does a builder quarry the needed stones by putting one stone into place and then going away to quarry, cut and shape another, and so on? No; he sees to it the material he needs is on the ground before the building is commenced, or at least that such provision has been made so the material will be on hand just when he needs it for its proper place in the structure he is erecting. And is it not obvious that the more material the preacher has on hand and laid out before him when he is about to begin the preparation of his sermon, the greater the variety of illustrations and facts possible in his message? And will not his sermon preparation be facilitated thereby? The less of "special" reading and preparation there is for each sermon the better.

Chapter 7

ARRANGING SERMON
MATERIAL

THERE SHOULD BE NO QUESTION as to the great importance
of a proper arrangement of the sermon material. Very
often the only difference between a sermon great in power
and one lacking in power is a difference in the arrangement. Some sermons remind us of the account of the dawn
of creation as recorded in chapter 1 of Genesis: "without
form, and void." The story is told of an old man who was
a regular church attendant and who always pitched the
tunes at prayer meeting. The hymnbook used contained
the words of the hymns but not the music. This regular
attendant was depended upon to start the hymn. One
night one of the elders gave out a new hymn; he said it
was a beautiful hymn, and he wished they could sing it.
The old chorister called out, "What is the meter, brother?"
The elder replied, "It ain't got no meter." And about as
much can be said of many a sermon—it is minus arrangement.

Lack of and carelessness in the matter of arrangement is
one of the most common faults of preaching today. It
ought to be considered inexcusable, because it implies a
lack of labor and an unwillingness to spend time on the

sermon. Laziness is a sin many preachers need to repent of and forsake.

Rousseau said that when writing a love letter, "You should begin without knowing what you are going to say and end without knowing what you have said." This may be good advice as to the writing of love letters, but it is certainly fatal advice when applied to sermon preparation.

The preacher is somewhat of an architect; it is his business to erect a structure out of the material he has on hand. Out of the same material can be built a prison, a stable, a mansion, or a palace. Which shall be built depends altogether on the arrangement of the material. The preacher may also be likened to an army general who distributes his regiments in different places but with one objective point. The preacher ought to arrange his material so it will all converge to the one main purpose of the sermon. To some men the matter of arrangement comes somewhat natural; to others, and possibly to most, it is the result of hard work. At any rate and at any cost every preacher ought to seek to excel in the arrangement of sermon material.

I. ADVANTAGES IN THE ARRANGEMENT OF SERMON MATERIAL

A. To the Preacher

Many preachers have great difficulty in memorizing their sermon notes. The reason for this lies in the fact that the notes lack arrangement. Clear arrangement involves clearly defined thought and yields a clear grasp of the subject. Whatever is clearly and logically arranged is easy to memorize—at least very much easier than matter that is without form or order.

B. To the Sermon

It matters a great deal as to the effectiveness of a sermon whether it is clearly thought out in the mind of the preacher. If a subject is misty and hazy in the preacher's mind and disorderly in arrangement in the sermon notes, it is almost an impossibility and requires a miracle of grace for the audience to get a clear grasp of the subject.

C. To the Audience

The audience is a great factor to consider in the matter of sermonizing. Whatever makes it easy for a congregation to remember and carry away the general plan and outline and consequently much of the content of a sermon is something not to be neglected by the preacher and is worth his constant toil to attain. It is absolutely certain the average audience can carry away a sermon that is well planned and arranged a thousand times better than one that is poorly arranged or has no arrangement at all. Good arrangement on the part of the preacher is absolutely necessary for good following on the part of the audience. Many an audience can truthfully say to the preacher: "We know not whither thou goest; and how can we know the way?" The preacher may imitate Abraham, who went out not knowing whither he went. But Abraham had a command for such conduct; the preacher has not. How often we hear this remark at the close of a sermon: "Oh, but we had a fine sermon today. I do not believe I ever heard a finer one." "Indeed," the other responds, "and what were the leading thoughts of the great sermon you heard?" "Oh, well," replies the first speaker, "I cannot tell you just what the chief points were, but it was a great sermon." Is not such a confession very often an indication of the lack of sermon arrangement on the part of the preacher? Specific thoughts were not clearly defined, consequently the hearer was not able to clearly define either the thoughts of the sermon or the obedience that should follow. The result of the sermon is, therefore, fleeting; it soon passes away and the place thereof knows it no more.

D. To the Theme

Is there not something due the theme or subject of the sermon in this matter of arrangement? Does not the theme cry out against injustice in this direction? Does it not rebel against chaotic treatment? Does it not demand that the material be arranged in order to be pleasing, convincing, and remembered by the audience? Assuredly it does.

II. CHARACTERISTICS AND QUALITIES OF A GOOD ARRANGEMENT

A. One Theme

One of the first lessons the preacher should learn is the importance of concentrating upon one theme in his sermon. It can justly be said of many sermons that they are composed of a series of homilies on various subjects. This is evident from the fact that a preacher, after he has been in the ministry some years, can examine his first sermons and find material enough in any one of them for four or five sermons on altogether different subjects. Herein lies a danger that besets expository preaching which must be constantly guarded against. The preacher should have only one theme in his sermon and concentrate all his argument, proof, testimony, illustration, and so on, toward the enforcing of that theme. If he finds himself wandering from the path of his stated theme, he must bring himself

back to it at all costs. Disobedience to this law is prac-
tically death to effectiveness in preaching. The exceptions
to this rule are not numerous enough to invalidate it.

B. A Logical Connection and Sequence between the Divisions of a Sermon

It is out of place to exhort before one instructs, or to
apply before one explains. First the seed, then the blade,
then the ear, then the full corn in the ear. The argument
should first be made to the intellect before the appeal to the
emotions and through them to the will. Let there be first
the negative, then the positive; the abstract, then the concrete; the general, then the particular.

C. Proper Emphasis to Various Parts of a Sermon

Which line of thought shall have the most prominent
place in the sermon depends altogether on the theme and
purpose of the sermon. Yet all the parts of a sermon, both
major and minor, must bear a symmetrical relation the
one to the other and to the whole.

III. THE ARRANGEMENT ITSELF

It is conceded that *a sermon needs an outline* just as a
man needs a skeleton. It has been said, "Sometimes Providence makes man without a bony skeleton, though even
then the place is occupied by cartilage." Sometimes sermons are made without a skeleton or even a cartilage. A
minister who had preached one of these sermons said to
his elder, after the close of the service, "Do you know I did
not know what I was to preach about when I went into the
pulpit this morning?" The elder was honest and replied,
"Do you know that no one knew what you had preached
about when you had finished?" The preacher is dealing

with the human mind, and its operations are subject to immutable laws as much as the stars. Rhetoric is not a human invention for the annoyance of students.

Generally speaking, the plan of a sermon should be *easy to follow*—particularly for the audience. Nor should it be so arranged as to become a weekly stereotyped thing. It was said of a preacher that when he had announced his first point, it was easy to tell what the remaining points were, for they were always the same. The power of reserve, surprise, and unexpectedness must be manifest in the arrangement as well as in the delivery of a sermon. Outlines that are striking are easily remembered. Some preachers, for this reason, make their outline so each general heading begins with the same word or sound. Others use the law of opposites and contrasts. A sermon preached some time ago had these headings: Theme—The Transfiguration: I. Place; II. Purpose; III. Persons; IV Power. Another: Theme—How to Become a Christian: I. Admit; II. Commit; III. Submit; IV. Transmit.

Chapter 8

INTRODUCTION OF THE SERMON

EVERY GOOD AND FINISHED SERMON or message divides itself into three parts: the introduction, the body or argument, and the conclusion.

It seems natural and fitting that a sermon or message should have an introduction. Just as our acquaintance with a friend is preceded by an introduction, so ought a sermon to be introduced. An introduction to a sermon is like a porch to a house—it would look unfinished without it. It is not without significance that every well written book has its preface, and every oratorio its prelude. Abrupt beginnings are to be avoided, because they are unnatural.

Of course, there are exceptions to this rule, as, for instance, when all the allotted time is necessary for the development of the sermon proper, when it may be deemed best to plunge at once into the subject without any stated introduction. Again, an informal talk, such as a prayer-meeting message, may not require an introduction. However, as a general rule it is best to introduce the subject.

I. THE PURPOSE OF AN INTRODUCTION

Why is an introduction to a sermon needed? In answer to this question we reply:

A. To Awaken an Interest in the Theme

It is not to be taken for granted that the people who listen to a sermon are automatically interested in it. This is by no means the situation. Some do not, others cannot, not a few will not manifest an interest in the theme presented. Yet, every public speaker knows that if he is to impress the minds and hearts of his hearers with the truth of his message, he must get them interested in what he is saying at all costs. If this interest is not secured at the outset, the probabilities are it will not be secured at all throughout the sermon. To fail to secure the ears of an audience is to fail to secure their minds. If their interest is obtained at the beginning, there is a good possibility of maintaining it to the end.

A good introduction is intended to arouse such an interest. An audience will not be interested simply because the speaker says, "Now hear me," or "Give me your attention," or "Now listen." It is the business of the public speaker to present his matter so interestingly that the audience cannot help but listen and be interested. So one of the purposes of an introduction is to awaken the interest of the audience in your theme.

B. To Prepare the Audience for What Is to Follow

It is an introduction to the theme. We are introduced to our friends for the purpose of further acquaintance. Introductions are of value only as they lead to this end. They are not for the present moment only; they have a relation to something further on. In other words, an introduction is a means to an end.

This leads to a caution: The preacher must not attempt to put all his sermon into the introduction. We have all probably at some time or other been introduced to some person who revealed his entire self in the first interview. Such people are not usually interesting. As a rule, people like to be kept anticipating for a while. Let no one make this mistake in preaching. The preacher who thrusts his sermon into his introduction is guilty of the same error. It must be remembered that the introduction to a sermon or message stands in the same relation to that composition as the introduction to a friend does to further friendship— it prepares the congregation for what is to follow.

II. THE SOURCES OF AN INTRODUCTION

What are the sources of an introduction, and of what material may it be composed? We may speak of eight sources:

A. The Text

Quite frequently the best material for an introduction will be found in the text itself.

1. Its Construction

If the text chosen is Ephesians 1:3-14, the theme of which is "Thanksgiving for the Blessings of Redemption," a fitting introduction will be found in the construction of the text. Close observation will reveal the fact that this thanksgiving assumes the form of a hymn of praise to the Trinity—the Father, the Son, and the Holy Spirit. It will further be noticed that these verses divide themselves naturally into a hymn of three stanzas, one being associated with the person and work of each of the three persons of the Godhead, and each closing with the same doxology: "to the praise of His glory." The work of the Father is set forth in verses 3-6, ending with a doxology; the work of the Son, verses 7-12, ending with a similar doxology; and the work of the Spirit, verses 13-14, also ending with the same doxology. It is thus evident that an interesting introduction can be made from the construction of the text.

2. FROM THE GENERAL FAMILIARITY WITH THE TEXT OR THEME

If one desires to preach a sermon from Psalm 23:4, "Yea, though I walk through the valley of the shadow of death," and so on, he may recall to the minds of the audience how many deathbeds have been lighted up with this text and how many thousands of hearts have found divine comfort from its words in the hour of death. Thus the general familiarity with the words of the text will undoubtedly prove an interesting introduction.

3. TO AVOID HAVING THE TEXT MISUNDERSTOOD

A sermon preached not long ago on the text Matthew 5:48, "Be ye therefore perfect," and so on, had the theme "Perfection in Love." The message was characterized by a splendid introduction based on the fact of the misunderstanding of the text. The preacher showed that instead of being a proof text for the much abused doctrine of sinless perfection, these words had reference only—and if not exclusively, certainly primarily—to perfection in love as shown in our attitude toward our enemies. To such perfection we may all attain. This was proven by referring to the context (vv. 43-47) which has special reference to the Christian's treatment of his enemies.

B. The Context

Take Hebrews 7:25, "Wherefore he is able to save them to the uttermost," and so on, as an example. A careful consideration of the context of this verse will reveal that Christ's ability to save the greatest sinners is not the theme taught in this verse. On the contrary, by virtue of the eternity of His priesthood as contrasted with the limited life service of the Levitical priests, He has power to finish and perfect the work already begun in the saints. Thus the context provides interesting as well as instructive material for an introduction. (See also p. 39)

C. The Historical Setting

An interesting introduction may be made for the theme "The Vision of Isaiah" (Isa. 6) by referring to the moral and political conditions of the time in which the prophet Isaiah lived (II Chron. 26). The principal events may be recalled: King Uzziah's wonderful reign; Isaiah's danger of attributing Israel's prosperity to the power of the king rather than to Jehovah; the pride and sin of the king; the death of the king, who was Isaiah's idol; then the prophet's vision, in which he saw *also* the Lord, another and greater King, the King of Glory, as supreme.

D. The Geography of the Bible

A description of the mountain, plain, sea, or city in which the words were spoken or the event transpired forms a good introduction. Such material is helpful for sermons on such topics as the transfiguration, the temptation, and the death of Christ.

E. The Customs and Antiquities of the Bible

An audience is always interested in the habits and customs of the peoples of other countries. The mode of dress, manner of living, customs of trade, habits of society, oriental marriages and funerals—these topics furnish instructive as well as interesting material for an introduction.

F. The Circumstances Peculiar to the Writer and Those Addressed

A recent sermon on "Glimpses of Paul's Inner Life," based on the letter to Philemon, had as its introduction a statement of the Apostle's relation to Philemon, his friend and a slaveowner. One of Philemon's slaves, Onesimus, had run away from his master, had heard Paul preach in Rome, was converted, and, desiring to return to his master, requested of the Apostle a letter of introduction to his Christian master and Paul's friend. Thus arose the occasion of the Epistle to Philemon.

G. The Occasion

A sermon preached at Easter could have no better introduction than one which referred to the universal commemoration of the resurrection of Christ. The same is true of Passion Week, Christmas, or any special occasion. The subject at a cottage prayer meeting may be introduced by mentioning that some of the greatest spiritual movements of history had their origin in a home prayer meeting. The value of education or present-day advantages along educational lines would furnish fitting material for an introduction to a baccalaureate address. When addressing an open-air gathering, one could conveniently declare that Christ did most of His preaching in the open air and presumably secured most of His disciples through open-air preaching.

H. The Subject

1. Its Pertinency to the Times

Mention of financial panics through which the country

has passed or may now be passing will form a good introduction to a sermon on the text: "Lay not up for yourselves
treasures upon earth." Someone preached a great sermon
on "The Instability of Earthly Things" some time ago,
using for his introduction reference to an earthquake that
had taken place in Sicily a few days before. So recent a
catastrophe made the introduction to the sermon very
effective.

2. The Disadvantages Which Come from Lack of Familiarity with the Subject

Some time ago the newspapers recorded a very sad
accident that occurred to a boy. The little fellow was
visiting his grandparents in a small city near Chicago
through which the electric railway passed. The boy came
from a rural district and had more than once amused himself by walking along the rails of the railroad tracks, so he
thought he would like to see how far he could walk on the
third rail of the electric road. Unfortunately he was ignorant of the danger hidden in the third rail. He stepped on
the rail, and the result was instant death. So ignorance of
one's subject may be attended with serious results.

3. The Advantages Which Come from Familiarity with the Text—the Converse Truth

4. The Utility of the Subject

Ephesians 6:5-9, the relation of masters to servants, as
setting forth a solution of the problems between capital
and labor, may be utilized as introductory material.

III. THE NEGATIVE QUALITIES OF A GOOD INTRODUCTION

A. No Boasting

Some preachers promise a good deal more in the introduction to the sermon than they are able to fulfill in the sermon proper. It is not right to arouse expectations at the beginning which one is unable to meet. Many preachers leave the preparation of the introduction until after the sermon proper is finished so they may not be guilty of this fault—a suggestion that young preachers may well heed and follow.

B. Not Too Loud, Sensational, or Emotional

The preacher should not begin in a loud tone of voice or in a sensational manner. It is too soon to make an appeal to the emotions or to attempt to touch the sympathetic chord. It is best to begin by speaking slowly and in a low tone of voice, warming up to the subject gradually, then working up to a climax.

C. Not Too Long

On opening a book, if one is confronted with a preface covering some twenty or thirty pages, he is likely to become discouraged and lay the book down. An old Scotch woman, whose pastor was guilty of consuming too much time in the introductions to his sermons, remarked, "The good old man takes so long a time setting the table and getting things ready that I lose my appetite by the time the meal comes." A lengthy introduction tires the people. One must not keep the people waiting too long on the porch, but let them into the house as soon as possible to see its furniture and enjoy its comforts. An introduction lasting five minutes is long enough for a forty-minute sermon.

IV. THE POSITIVE QUALITIES OF A GOOD INTRODUCTION

A. A Vital Relation to the Theme

B. Only One Theme

C. A Natural Transition

The transition from the introduction to the body of the sermon should be a natural one. It must not be forced, abrupt or strained.

D. Carefully Prepared

It should not be left to the spur of the moment or to the inspiration of the occasion. It is well to write it out fully. First impressions are the more lasting; therefore one must prepare the introduction well. It is not sufficient to write the word "Introduction" at the head of the sermon and do nothing further by way of preparation.

Chapter 9

BODY OF THE SERMON

THIS PART OF A SERMON has been called the plan or argument. As such, it implies that much thought and time should be spent upon it. The old adage, "If you think twice before you speak once, you will speak twice the better for it," is truly applicable here. However, one must be careful lest the plan or argument, although good and important in itself, be made a hobby and thus become burdensome, hindering rather than helping freeness and enthusiasm in delivery.

I. THE NUMBER OF DIVISIONS

This question has met with varied answers. Even good preachers differ among themselves in this regard, some advocating as many as seven, and others insisting on not more than three headings. It is doubtless true that no one man can be a law unto another in this respect. Each man must find out for himself by experience just how many or how few divisions he can most effectively divide his sermons into so as not to impede ease and freeness. Blind imitation is fatal here.

Such a saying as "Three heads, like a sermon" indicates that this number has been a generally accepted one. Just why this has been so we may not be able to state; nevertheless, an examination of the sermons of not a few great preachers reveals a preference for this number. The reason

may be because three divisions are not burdensome to remember for either preacher or people; they suggest a
beginning, a middle, and an end, afford variety, and avoid
tediousness. The preacher must not be bound in the matter;
he may use as many divisions as the topic calls for, the
subject will allow, and he can handle.

II. THE GENERAL NATURE OF THESE DIVISIONS

A. Not Too Prominent

The pulpit is neither a lecture room nor a dissecting
room. There is no particular beauty in a skeleton—even
though it be a sermon skeleton. The more flesh you can
put on it and the less the bony structure can be seen, the
more pleasing and inviting will be the sermon.

B. Setting Forth the Subject in a Full, Definite, and Clear Manner

This should particularly be the case when the subject
is not very clear from the text.

C. Natural and Logical in Their Order and Transition from One to Another

The negative must come before the positive, and the
primary before the secondary. It is not so much a matter
of finding a place for the divisions, but of finding the best
place for them—that is the important question to settle.

As to whether the outline shall be announced in advance, or each point named as it is reached, or whether
the divisions should be mentioned from the pulpit at all,
is a question on which there is much difference of opinion.
It is very helpful, particularly if the line of thought is
somewhat intricate and hard to follow, to draw attention

to the divisions as a help to the audience in its attempt to follow the thought of the sermon. On the other hand, some preachers think it takes away from the interest, freshness, and expectancy of the subject if the outline is announced beforehand. The question must be answered by each preacher according as he thinks he is best enabled to effectively present his message. Practice, observation, and inquiry will undoubtedly answer the question in each particular case.

The divisions of a sermon are for the purpose of elaborating and amplifying the subject. This may be done by restating the theme in different words, by detailing general statements, by setting forth abstract facts in concrete terms, and by clarifying the subject by the use of illustrations.

Let us now look at the particular nature of these divisions.

III. THE PARTICULAR NATURE OF THESE DIVISIONS

A. What?

The first division of a sermon should deal with a statement and definition of the subject or proposition. It should answer the question, What? It should occupy itself with definitions and should afford the preacher the opportunity of stating clearly and unmistakably just what is the theme he is dealing with and what the particular phase of the doctrine or duty he is inculcating. There should be no misunderstanding of the subject after the first division is thoroughly dealt with. The deck should then be clear for action. It is in a very special sense an address to the intellect as contrasted with that to the emotions or the will.

But how can we answer this sermon question, What?
In four ways:

1. Definition of the Subject and Its Terms

For instance, if the theme of the sermon is "Sanctification," then the purpose of the first division should be to
define just what is meant by this word. Here one may
deal with misunderstood phases of the subject, refute errors, correct erroneous views, and set forth in clear outline
just what is meant by the term "sanctification."

The subject may be elucidated by setting forth the synonymous terms in which this doctrine is stated, or by
setting forth its relation to the other great doctrines of
the Scriptures, such as justification or regeneration. Here
one clearly defines the meaning of the words and terms
of the theme. This is the part of the sermon in which much
use is made of the dictionary and lexicon.

2. Explanation

The text is often misunderstood. An example: "But as
it is written, Eye hath not seen, nor ear heard, neither
have entered into the heart of man, the things which God
hath prepared for them that love him" (I Cor. 2:9). How
often we hear this verse applied to the future glory of the
believer, whereas it actually has no reference to the future
at all, as verse 10 clearly shows: "But God hath [now]
revealed them unto us by his Spirit." This is what is meant
by explanation.

Let the preacher be sure what he is seeking to explain
is really explainable. It is questionable, to say the least,
whether some of the doctrines of the Christian faith are
really explainable: for example, the Trinity is a fact of the
Christian faith to be believed, not a doctrine to be ex-

plained. Before undertaking to explain any subject, one must be sure he understands it himself. These words of warning may not be out of place, for more than one preacher has been guilty of the folly of seeking to explain some difficult subject, at the same time manifesting to his audience how totally ignorant he himself was of it.

3. COMPARISONS, RELATIONS, AND CONTRASTS

How often Christ defined such terms as "the kingdom of heaven" by likening it to something already familiar to his hearers: "The kingdom of heaven is like unto a net that was cast into the sea, and gathered of every kind." The preacher will do well to ask, with the great Teacher, "To what shall I liken" this? In what better way could the doctrine of the imminence of the second coming of Christ have been set forth than by the words "like a thief"? Preachers make the mistake of not putting enough "likes" in their sermons. To define the subject, therefore, one must ask himself to what he should liken it.

Or one may seek to show how his subject is related to kindred subjects: for example, if "Justification" is his theme, he might explain how it is related to sanctification and adoption.

Or, again, it may be asked, To what does this truth stand in contrast? Scripture makes much use of this method of definition: for example, sheep and goats, wheat and chaff, light and darkness, godly and ungodly, saint and sinner, life and death. We learn the truth by contrast.

4. ILLUSTRATIONS

An illustration is to a sermon what a window is to a

building—that which lets light in. A house must not be all windows, nor must a sermon be all illustrations. While the power of illustration is subject to abuse, it nevertheless is one of the most effective means for defining words, terms, or subjects. One must be very sure that the illustration really illustrates. Stained glass windows do not let in much light. The parables of Christ are the illustrations of His subjects. How forcibly the foolishness of the man who hears the word and does not obey it is set forth by the illustration of the man who built his house upon the sand (Matt. 7). How vividly the folly of riches is set forth by the story of the rich fool (Luke 12:16-21).

To sum up then, we may say that the purpose of the first division of the body or plan of a sermon is to clearly, fully, and lucidly set forth the theme of the sermon by definition, explanation, comparison, relation contrast, and illustration.

B. Why?

This division should seek to answer the question, Why? It should endeavor to set forth the necessity, reason, or proof of the theme or proposition. If the first division asks, What is the subject? the second asks, Why is it true? Why should I believe it or accept it? How may it be proven? Is it reasonable?

All things are not to be taken for granted. The acceptance of some facts rests upon evidence. Christ gave "many infallible proofs" of His resurrection.

It should be remembered that not everything needs to be proven; some facts are self-evident. It is not necessary to attempt to prove the sun exists, for it is a self-evident fact. Nor need one enter into an argument to prove the existence of God. The evidences of His handiwork are too apparent: "The invisible things of him from the creation of the world are clearly seen." "The heavens declare the glory of God." Again, not everything can be proven: the doctrine of the Trinity, for example. Nor must one consider himself under obligation to prove a negative. If "the fool hath said in his heart, There is no God," then it is his duty to prove there is none, not the Christian's to prove there is. One should not attempt to prove a thing which he himself does not believe to be true or capable of proof. Herein lies one of the serious dangers of accepting, for the purpose of debate, that phase of a subject which he does not believe nor deem capable of proof. If one is satisfied that a thing is not true nor capable of proof, then he should not undertake to prove its truthfulness.

Another word by way of suggestion: The preacher should begin his argument by using some fact already known to and acknowledged by the hearer. Let him argue from the known to the unknown, using familiar arguments. Paul, when arguing with farmers, spoke to them of "fruitful seasons"; but when addressing the Athenian philosophers, he referred them to what their "own poets" had said. The common people heard Christ gladly because He used arguments they could readily understand. It is well for the preacher to rely, as far as possible, upon scriptural arguments, for they are the most convincing.

The following are the most common sources of argument:*

1. CAUSE AND EFFECT

Briefly stated, this means that every effect has some cause. Nothing is without cause. If one is seeking to prove the resurrection of Christ, he may use such arguments as

*Cf. Broadus, *Preparation and Delivery of Sermons.*

the empty grave, the Lord's day, the Christian Church. These are effects; what are their causes? How did that tomb become empty? What accounts for the change from the Jewish Sabbath to the Christian Lord's day? What gave rise to the Christian Church? In what great fact did the New Testament have its birth? On what ground has the Christian Church for centuries commemorated the Easter festival? These are effects; what are their causes?

2. Testimony

Much use can be made of this method of argument in such texts as: "What think ye of Christ? whose son is he?" What was the testimony of those who were closest to Him and knew Him best? What did His enemies say about Him? What was the testimony of His works?

Effective testimony is said to depend upon three things: First, the character of a witness. Therefore, lawyers seek to impeach the character of the witness in order that his testimony may have an unfavorable effect upon the jury. A witness whose integrity is beyond question is far more valuable in proving a case than one whose character and reputation are open to suspicion. Second, the number of the witnesses. The fact that twenty men witnessed an accident, which they attributed to carelessness on the part of an engineer, is more convincing to a jury than the testimony of only five, or even ten, who testified to the contrary. How does this bear upon the testimony of Christ's resurrection? Was He not "seen of above five hundred brethren at once"? Third, the character of the fact borne witness to. An ordinary fact does not need so great an amount of testimony for its proof as an extraordinary fact does. A supernatural fact needs much stronger evidence for its proof than a natural fact does. The testimony to the supernatural fact of Christ's life received heavenly or supernatural witness and testimony (II Peter 1:16-18).

The testimony of enemies is specially valuable. Hence the testimony of Josephus, Judas Iscariot, Pilate, and demons to Christ's person and work is exceedingly important.

3. AUTHORITY

Foremost in this respect is the authority of the Scriptures. In matters of faith and Christian practice the Bible is the court of final appeal, the ultimate authority. The opinion of scholars, the "generally received opinions of mankind, and the proverbs and maxims which express the collective judgment of many, have a greater or less authority according to the nature of the case. . . . Proverbs, or what the common people call 'old sayings,' are very often, as it has been remarked, but the striking expression of some half truth, or the result of some hasty generalization, and in many cases they can be matched by other sayings to precisely the opposite effect." Therefore, great care should be exercised in the choice of such authorities or so-called authoritative sayings.

4. INDUCTION

Induction has been defined as "the process of a general rule from a sufficient number of particular cases. Finding something to be true of certain individual objects, we conclude that the same thing is true of the whole class to which these individuals belong, and afterward prove it to be true of any new object, simply by showing that that object belongs to the same class." This form of argument is said to be the commonest and fraught with the greatest error and danger if not properly used. Obviously, the greatest care should be exercised in its use.

5. Analogy

Logically speaking, an analogy is "a form of reasoning, from the similarity of two or more things in certain particulars; their similarity in other particulars is inferred. Thus, the earth and Mars are both planets, nearly equidistant from the sun, not differing greatly in density, having similar distributions of seas and continents, alike in conditions of humidity, temperature, seasons, day and night, etc., but the earth also supports organic life; hence Mars (probably) supports organic life—is an argument from analogy"—*Century Dictionary.* If men say it would be unjust of God to punish them for violating His law when they did not believe or certainly did not know it was His law, we point out to them that this holds true of physical laws—he who takes poison will be killed, even though he did not know or did not believe it was poison. If men object to the doctrine of original sin as incompatible with divine goodness, we can point to inherited disease, inherited inclinations to vice, inherited dishonor.

6. Deduction

Deduction is the inverse process of inferring a particular case from a law of cases presumed to be of like nature; something derived as a result from a known fact; a necessary inference. Suppose we say of a man, "He cannot help taking gloomy views of life, because his health is so poor." Here is an argument based on the general assumption that any one whose health is poor must take gloomy views of life. "This invention will not come into extensive use; it is cumbrous, hard to operate, and liable to get out of order." Here the reasons given all help to firmly fix the assertion, being based on the general truth that any machine that is cumbrous, hard to operate, and liable to get out of order is impaired for extensive use.

7. REFUTATION

The preacher must "be able by sound doctrine both to exhort and to convince the gainsayers. For there are many unruly and vain talkers and deceivers . . . whose mouths must be stopped" (Titus 1:9-11). Refuting doubtless comes more easy to men than proving, inasmuch as it is easier to pull down than it is to build up. The preacher must not undertake to refute every objection to the truth. Some objections are not worth refuting. Nor must he create objections for the purpose of refuting them. Refutation, whether of an erroneous proposition or of an objection to the truth, will be accomplished by showing either that the terms are ambiguous, the premises false, the reasoning unsound, or the conclusion irrelevant. Refutation of an error is sometimes strengthened by showing how the error may have originated. Our Lord made use of this form of argument in Matthew 12:27: "If I by Beelzebub cast out devils, by whom do your children cast them out?" In refuting one should state the objection fully and fairly so that the hearer will be able to say, "Yes, that is a full and fair statement of the case; if that can be answered satisfactorily, it will help me."

8. EXPERIENCE

Paul appealed to this in his great argument for the resurrections of Christ (I Cor. 15). The Apostle declared: "If Christ be not raised, your faith is vain; ye are yet in your sins" (v. 17). But the Corinthians knew they had not believed in vain. They knew by a very real experience they were not still in their sins, for a power, far greater than any human power or self-imposed reformation and which must, therefore, have come from the risen Christ, had given them a glorious victory over their previous sinful life. An answered prayer is the best argument for the reality of prayer. It is Christian experience that has saved Christian doctrine, not vice versa. The strongest argument for the existence of God and the deity of Christ lies in the Christian experience of these facts.

Sometimes the second general division of a sermon occupies itself with showing the *necessity* or the *reasonableness* of the theme discussed. For illustration of this usage, see the sermons on "The New Birth" and "The Resurrection of Jesus Christ" (pp. 127 and 125).

C. How?

The purpose of this division is to set forth the manner and method by which the theme of the sermon may be brought about or the conditions under which it may be received or fulfilled. If the theme of discussion is "Regeneration," for example, and the two divisions already dealt with have shown what this doctrine means and why it is necessary, then the third division shows how it may be brought about: what it is; why it is; how it takes place.

There are three thoughts usually present in the treatment of this division: the divine agency, or God's part; the human agency, or man's part; the question of means. For illustration, see the outline of the sermon on "The New Birth" (p. 127).

D. What Then?

The first division answers the question, What? by ex-

planation; the second, Why? by argumentation; the third,
How? by what means; the fourth, What then? by applica-
tion. What is it? Why is it? How is it? What then?
These are the four divisions of the body or argument of a
sermon. (See sermon outline on "The Resurrection of Jesus
Christ," p. 125.)

This part of the sermon is by no means to be considered
subordinate or a mere addition to the composition. Indeed,
it may be questioned whether the sermon proper has really
begun until the application is reached. The late Charles
H. Spurgeon said, "Where the application begins, there
the sermon begins." Daniel Webster remarked on one occasion, "When a man preaches to me, I want him to make
it a personal matter, a personal matter, a personal matter!"
The application is that part of the sermon which more than
any other part makes it a personal matter.

Many preachers form the habit of making a practical
application after each point in the sermon. This will naturally have some modifying effect upon this particular division. And yet, it does seem perfectly fitting and natural
that there should be a practical application of the whole
matter at the conclusion of the sermon. Therefore, if application is made at the end of each division it may be well
not to make it exhaustive, but to leave sufficient to make a
fitting close to the sermon.

1. THE APPLICATION MAY ASSUME VARIOUS FORMS:

a. Instruction

For example, if the theme of the sermon is "The Need
of Bible Study," a fitting application would consist in the
giving instruction as to how to proceed to the study of
the Bible. In the first part of the sermon the preacher has
set forth very clearly just what is meant by Bible study,

and in the second, convincing reasons why the Bible should be studied. It seems only natural and proper that he should now give instruction as to how this study can be carried on so as to yield the best results. Many a preacher has sent his audience away convinced and longing, but ignorant of the best way or any way of satisfying that longing. This is wrong.

b. Persuasion

Dr. Broadus says, "It is not enough to convince men of truth, nor enough to make them see how it applies to themselves, and how it might be practicable for them to act it out—but we must persuade men." A distinguished minister said he could never exhort; he could explain and prove what was truth and duty, but then he must leave the people to themselves. The Apostle Paul, however, could not only argue, but could also say, "We pray you in Christ's stead, be ye reconciled to God." From observation and experience it is obvious that a man may see his duty and still neglect it. We have often been led by persuasion to do something, good or bad, from which we are shrinking. It is not enough that men *see* the truth; they must be made to *feel* it. Men usually do not turn from sin simply because they ought to. They must be made to feel the awfulness and the guilt of it before they will turn away from it. In other words, they must be persuaded it is to their best and eternal interests to forsake sin. Men become wearied of constant exhortations; they must be made to feel.

2. Action and Emotion

Therefore, the preacher ought to know *the link which connects action with feeling*. He must study the emotions.

The will is not a self-determining factor. It does not act independently of the emotions, but is moved to action by them. Desire naturally prompts volition.

"Reason, reason, as much as you like; but beware of thinking that it answers for everything. This mother loves her child; will reason comfort her? Does cool reason control the inspired poet, the heroic warrior, the lover? Reason guides but a small part of man, and that the least interesting. The rest obeys feeling, true or false; and passion, good or bad."—ABBE ROUX

If the preacher is deficient in this power, he ought to cultivate it; if excessive, restrain it. He ought to study some authoritative work on the subject.

3. IMPELLING MOTIVES

Particular attention ought also to be paid to the motives that lead men to action. The preacher should be a master in handling them. "Impelling motives," says Professor A. E. Phillips in his work *Effective Speaking*, "may be defined as man's spiritual, intellectual, moral and material wants. For working purposes they may be given the following classification: Self-preservation, property, power, reputation, affection, sentiments, tastes. The distinction between these impelling motives and the manner of their application may be seen best, perhaps, by an example. Let us suppose the purpose is to have the listener lead a temperate life. The argument, in outline, might consist of the entire Seven Impelling Motives, after the manner following:

Theme: You should be temperate in all things—because you will be better off from the following viewpoints:

Self-Preservation. You will have better health and a longer life.

Property. You will earn more and save more.

Power. You will have greater mental force, greater moral power, greater self-control. You will do more yourself and exert greater power over others.

Reputation. Your friends and acquaintances will admire you, hold you in higher esteem.

Affections. You will avoid wounding the feelings of those you love; your companionship will give them greater pleasure. You will be able to be of more use to them.

Sentiments. You will prove yourself a man. You will show self-respect. It is right to be temperate.

Tastes. You will increase both your opportunity and your ability to appreciate the best in art, literature, drama.

If, then, we are seeking action so frequently, and, if, further, action is the result of the superiority of the impelling motives over the restraining motives, it is plain that the more we bring these impelling motives to bear upon a given audience or person, the more likely will we attain our end. Therefore, it is of the greatest importance that we master their ready use."

The preacher, of course, dealing as he does with eternal issues, will deal with the spiritual and eternal phases of these impelling motives. Under "Self-preservation" he will deal not merely with "better health and a longer life" here but with the eternal life of the ages to come. Under "Reputation" he will speak not only of the admiration of friends and acquaintances but of what is infinitely more important —the esteem and approval of God.

Chapter 10

CONCLUSION OF THE SERMON

I. ITS IMPORTANCE

THE GREEK ORATORS expressed their conception of the importance of the conclusion of an address or oration by calling it "the final struggle which decides the conflict." It is not too much to say that the last five minutes of the sermon is the most important part of it. It is during this time that the issues involved are decided, if decided at all. Yet, how very seldom the conclusion receives the preparation and thought it ought to by virtue of its important place. Very often its matter and form are left to the inspiration (?) of the moment. How scattering, wild, and pointless are the "concluding remarks" of the average sermon—what aimless exhortations! This is sad, indeed, when we remember the preacher has been speaking for thirty or forty minutes for the very purpose of accomplishing the work of the last five minutes. The introduction and the body or argument of the sermon, with its definition, explanation, proof, and argument, have all been dealt with for the very purpose of bringing things to an issue in the conclusion. What a mistake to neglect the thorough preparation of this important part of the sermon.

II. WHAT FORM SHALL THE CONCLUSION TAKE?

The answer to this question depends altogether on the manner in which the matter which may properly belong to the conclusion has been included in the preceding part —What then?—of the sermon. If the main issue of the conclusion is to leave the listener with the impression of completeness, then it may be well to gather up the missing threads. This is sometimes done by what is called:

A. Recapitulation

Cicero defines "recapitulation" as "recollection revived, not speech repeated." By this we are to understand that to repeat the divisions or leading thoughts of the sermon is not a breach of homiletics but that recapitulation must not consist merely in such repetition. It should rather take the form of a grand resumé in which is gathered up in a few striking, well-chosen, soul-moving sentences, or in a well-chosen and pointed illustration, the grand, central idea and purpose of the entire sermon.

B. Poem or Illustration

Sometimes the conclusion of the sermon takes the form of a poem or the verse of some well-known hymn. Or the sermon may be finished by the use of one striking sentence.

(Under "The Application May Assume Various Forms" there are further instructions on this point, pp. 85, 86.)

III. WHAT SHOULD BE THE LENGTH OF THE CONCLUSION?

It should not be any longer than the introduction. From three to five minutes is long enough. The preacher should conclude when he is through. If he says, "And now, finally," let it be finally. He must not say, "Now, this last word," and then still go on. If it is the last word, let it be the last. Indeed it may not be wise to let it be known that he is bringing his sermon to a close. It is better to close before his people think about it. It is better to leave a congregation longing than loathing.

There are illustrations of textual sermons on pp. 125-141.

Chapter 11

EXPOSITORY SERMONS

IT IS SURPRISING how many preachers concede the exceedingly important place that ought to be given to expository preaching in their ministry and then confess in almost the same breath that they do not give it such a place. They admit they ought to do it and concurrently confess they do not. Just why they do not follow the expository method of preaching is not quite clear. Many feel they do not possess the ability for it, that they do not have the gift of an expositor. Ought not the preacher to cultivate and stir up such a gift? Should he not preach after this manner as well as after any other? If he admits expository preaching is one of the best methods of preaching, if not the very best, ought he not to learn to preach in that way? If one is afraid to venture on this method at the regular Sunday services, experiment may be made in the midweek meeting. At all events it ought to be tried. F. B. Meyer and G. Campbell Morgan of London were both noted expository preachers.

I. DEFINITION OF EXPOSITORY SERMON

What is meant by an expository sermon, and in what respects does it differ from other sermons? Mainly because it is occupied more fully with the exposition of the Scripture itself than is the case with, for example, the textual sermon. The textual or topical sermon occupies itself chiefly with one certain thought or topic suggested by the text; whereas the expository sermon occupies itself with the exposition of the entire scripture chosen.

II. ADVANTAGES TO BE DERIVED FROM EXPOSITORY PREACHING

A. It Produces Biblical Preachers and Hearers

No preacher can adopt the expository method of proclaiming truth without himself being very greatly indoctrinated and enriched by the study of the Word. No congregation can sit long under a ministry of this kind without being deeply instructed in the Scriptures. Thus the preacher and his audience will be kept Biblical.

B. It Conforms to the Biblical Ideal of Preaching

It is more in harmony with the scriptural plan of preaching as illustrated, for example, in the Acts of the Apostles, than textual preaching. This was Jesus' method (Luke 4), Stephen's (Acts 7 and 8), Paul's (Acts 28), and Peter's (Acts 2 and 3).

C. It Is Wider in Scope

It affords the preacher a wider scope for the practical application of truth to the lives of his hearers. Too often the minister is accused of being too personal in his application of certain truth, going astray from his text in order to make personal references. Whether this is altogether true or not, it is a criticism often made in connection with the textual sermon. This criticism would either be altogether removed or greatly lightened if the expository method were pursued. It gives one greater opportunity for application.

III. THE POSSIBLE DISADVANTAGES OF EXPOSITORY PREACHING

Can there be dangers connected with so advantageous a form of preaching? Yes. They are to be guarded against to avoid seriously hurting one's ministry. Some of these possible disadvantages are:

A. It Can Become Monotonous for the Congregation

There is the danger that comes from announcing the same book of the Bible from which your text is taken for many successive Sundays. This is likely to create monotony with a consequent loss of interest and probably attendance. Yet one need not continue choosing his text from the same book week after week. Expository preaching does not necessarily involve any such course of action.

B. The Preacher Can Become Lazy

If not carefully watched, it may lead to laziness in the way of preparation of one's sermon. There is such a danger of reading verse after verse of the chosen text, passing a few comments or making a few remarks on them, so that the sermon becomes a little commentary on the passage chosen rather than a proclamation of the great truth set forth therein. As someone has well said, "If he is persecuted in one passage, he can flee to another."

C. The Text May Be Too Long

It is sometimes considered disadvantageous because the text chosen for consideration is so large it cannot be reasonably expected that the audience can remember it. This is definitely unfortunate as it would hinder reception of the message and would tend to discourage the memorizing of Scripture.

D. Such Preaching Is Too Confining

It has been said the expository method of preaching does not afford the opportunity for dealing with current topics. Yet the wide-awake preacher can make it minister to such needs.

IV. SUGGESTIONS FOR EXPOSITORY PREACHING

A. Let the Text Be a Portion of Scripture That Contains One Leading Thought or Theme

The expository sermon should be characterized by a unity of theme just as much as a textual sermon. Simply because there are many verses in the text is no reason why there should be many and different thoughts or themes, thus constituting a number of sermonettes in one sermon. It may be more difficult to find this unity of thought in expository than in textual preaching because of the difference in length of the text chosen, but to be successful in this method of preaching demands that it be done at all costs. It is this slipshod method of covering many themes in one sermon and calling it expository preaching that has brought this splendid and Biblical method of proclaiming the truth of God into disrepute in some quarters. The expository sermon must be characterized by unity of theme. In order to accomplish this desirable end, it can be readily seen, one cannot expound upon every detail in the text chosen.

B. Texts Should Be Chosen from Different Parts of the Scripture

To avoid the disadvantage of the monotony mentioned above, the preacher must not confine himself to one book in the Bible nor to successive chapters in the one book. To begin with, he should select certain important and well-known passages containing, perhaps, not more than four or five verses. Then he may take an entire paragraph, then a whole chapter. After a while, when the congregation has become accustomed to the expository method of preaching, he may choose a whole book, such as the Epistle to the Ephesians. He should not choose a book with too many chapters to begin with. It takes too long a time to finish the book, and the interest of the people is likely to lag in the meantime. The epistles to the Colossians, Titus, or the second one to the Thessalonians are good books to begin with.

C. A Thorough Study of the Entire Text Is an Absolute Condition of Success

Not only must the entire section be studied, but every paragraph, verse, sentence, phrase, and word must be carefully studied until its meaning is ascertained. Some have erroneously supposed that expository preaching is a lazy way of preaching. If anything, it requires far more work than any other method of sermonizing. But it yields larger results and so is worth the extra work. Sermonizing is hard and laborious work anyway. The true preacher will have no easy time of it. Lazy men had better steer clear of the ministry.

D. The Preacher Must Avoid Being Merely Theoretic; He Must Be Practical as Well

There is great danger in expository preaching of the preacher being so taken up with the great truths set forth in the text and with the endeavor to make others see them that he could forget that the end of all preaching is practice and so overlook the practical application of the great truths enunciated. Let him remember that where the application begins, the sermon begins. He must not fail to apply the truth taught.

Illustrations of expository sermons are on pp. 142-146.

Chapter 12

BIBLE READINGS

CONCISELY STATED, the difference between a Bible reading and a textual sermon lies in this: the former consists in the compilation of a greater or lesser number of Scripture passages and their comparison one with another, while the latter usually consists in the exposition of a single text.

I. ADVANTAGES OF A BIBLE READING OVER THE TEXTUAL SERMON

A. For the Preacher Himself

1. IT IS SIMPLER AND EASIER.

The complexity so characteristic of the textual sermon is for the most part absent in the Bible reading. Multiform divisions and minute analysis are not usually required. Therefore, it is a good style of preaching for the beginner in homiletics to adopt.

2. IT KEEPS HIS MIND FROM WANDERING.

The preacher is not confined to a single text. He cannot very well be accused of the fault into which the old country preacher is said to have fallen, namely, taking a text, then departing from it, and finally not coming back to it.

3. IT HELPS KEEP THE PREACHER BIBLICAL.

It is possible in the preparation of a textual sermon to

read the Bible for the text, then to close it and not look at it again during the preparation of the sermon. This is hardly possible in the preparation of a Bible reading, for one is compelled to constantly turn from one part of the Bible to another. Scripture must be compared with scripture. To do this means becoming a Biblical preacher.

4. IT HAS THE TENDENCY TO PREVENT ONE-SIDED VIEWS OF BIBLE TRUTHS.

One can scarcely fail to get a full-orbed view of the truth selected for the Bible reading as long as he is compelled to search from one end of the Bible to the other for his sermon material.

B. With Reference to the People

1. BY THIS STYLE OF PREACHING THE PEOPLE WILL CONTINUALLY BE INSTRUCTED IN DIVINE TRUTH

They will be likely to know much more of God's Word and will than by listening to textual sermons only. There is a sad lack of Bible instruction in the average sermon. Very often the only Biblical thing about the sermon is the text. If the sermonizing of the past few years had had a much greater supply of Bible instruction in it, the number of people who have left our churches and joined some of the misleading and erroneous sects would have been far less.

2. IT KEEPS THE PEOPLE IN A SPIRIT OF CONSTANT EXPECTANCY.

They will be wondering what is in reserve. They will be desirous of knowing what phase of the truth is to be presented next. This is also of great advantage to the preacher.

II. HELPS NEEDED IN THE CONSTRUCTION
OF BIBLE READINGS

A. Concordance

Among concordances Cruden's stands first and foremost
for those who study the Bible in English only and have no
knowledge of Greek or Hebrew. Strong's, Young's, and the
Englishman's Greek Concordance may be used very effectively by those who have a very little knowledge of the
Greek. Indeed, if one knows but the Greek and Hebrew
alphabet he can use these works with great profit and
with much advantage over Cruden's.

B. A Topical Textbook

There are two kinds of such books. One has the topics
arranged in their logical order, irrespective of their order
in the Bible, an example of which is Torrey's *New Topical Text Book*. The other contains the topics according
to their order in the Bible, of which Inglis' *Bible Text
Cyclopedia* is a good illustration. Each one has its own
particular advantage.

C. Word Lists

By these are meant such lists of topics and subjects as
will be found at the back of the ordinary teacher's Bible.

D. A Good, Well-bound Reference Bible

While mentioned last, this is the most important. What
is the best reference Bible? Opinions differ. One Bible
teacher likes one kind, another prefers some other. There
is as much difference among Bible teachers with reference
to the best edition of the Bible as there is among music
teachers concerning the best make of pianos. It is good

to have an American Standard Version as well as the Authorized Version to which you may continually refer. Some things are much clearer in the American Standard Version than in the King James Version. Other translations which one might consult include: The Berkeley Version, The Amplified Bible, the Charles B. Williams New Testament, and Wuest's Expanded Translation of the New Testament.

III. THE PLAN AND METHOD OF CONSTRUCTING BIBLE READINGS

Having chosen the theme for the Bible reading, the rules for which are the same as those which enter into the choice of a text for a textual sermon (see p. 23), the preacher should proceed in the following manner:

A. He Must Find Out the Teaching of the WHOLE Bible on the Subject Chosen

The Bible must be searched from Genesis to Revelation in order to obtain a full and complete view of the subject under consideration. Only thus may one-sidedness and hobby-riding be avoided. If he is to declare the whole counsel of God to the people he must know the whole counsel, and in order to know it he must know what the whole Bible says about it. This means that in preparing a Bible reading on "Faith," for example, he must look up not only all that is to be found under the word "faith," but also what is recorded under the synonyms for faith, such as "belief," "believe," "receive," "trust," and so on. This does not mean, of course, that one must read the Bible through from beginning to end in order to do this. The concordance may be used for this purpose.

B. He Should Prepare Sheets of Paper with Appropriate Headings

After preparing four or five sheets of blank paper, he should write on the top of the first sheet the question, What?; on the second, Why?; the third, How?; the fourth, What then? More sheets of paper may be used as the preparation may require.

C. Now He Will Take the Concordance, Which We Will Suppose in This Case is Cruden's

He will obviously turn first to the word "faith." The first thing to be found under this word is a number of definitions of the word. Various kinds of faith are mentioned, such as historical, temporary, justifying, and so on. These definitions with their accompanying references may be written down on the sheet of paper marked, What? This is for the purpose of defining the subject.

Coming more particularly to the work of the concordance proper one would read down the column until he comes, for example, to Hebrews 11:1—"Faith is the substance of things hoped for," and so on. Here is a definition of faith. He would write on the sheet marked, What? the following: "Heb. 11:1—Faith is the substance," and so on. Reading further in the concordance he would come to Hebrews 11:6—"Without faith it is impossible to please God." Where shall he put this? On what sheet? Under what heading? Under the question, Why? because it shows the necessity for having faith. Reading again, he comes to Romans 10:17—"Faith cometh by hearing," and so on. This verse may be written on the sheet marked, How? for it shows how faith may be obtained. The preacher proceeds in this way until he has finished every reference in the column of the concordance. The synonyms must then be examined and dealt with in the same way. Thus a thorough grasp of the subject as set forth in the whole Bible is obtained.

A word or two with reference to the use of the other concordances mentioned above may be helpful at this point. Let us take a glance at Strong's. As one allows his eye to pass from quotation to quotation in the column on "faith," he quickly observes that by the side of each reference there is a number which refers him to a glossary at the back of the book. He further observes that different numerals are placed opposite the various references, thus indicating that in the original the word is not just exactly the same in meaning. For instance, in looking up the meaning of the word "faith" in Romans 14:22 ("Hast thou faith?") one is surprised to find that the word here used does not mean "faith" in the generally accepted sense of that word at all. It does not mean saving faith, nor even that faith that lays hold of the promises of God, but simply "persuasion," thus making "Hast thou faith?" read, "Art thou persuaded?" Such an understanding of the words in the texts used is very important for a true presentation of the doctrine.

IV. BY WAY OF SUGGESTION AND CAUTION

A. One Must Not Use Too Many Texts of Scripture

No infallible rule can be laid down as to the number of Scripture passages to be used in any one Bible reading. Only the most striking and representative passages should be chosen. The length of comment made on each passage, together with the amount of time at the disposal of the speaker, will determine the number. Examine outlines of Bible readings on pp. 147-155.

B. He Should Arrange the Texts in Their Logical Order

Let progress in thought mark the order and arrangement of the references. The transition from one thought to another should be natural, not forced or strained.

C. He Should Explain Each Passage or Group of Passages

No pains should be spared in the minute analysis of each word in each verse chosen as a proof text. He must understand just what the text teaches. The explanation should be such as the audience can readily understand. See under "Interpretation of the Text," p. 32.

D. He Should Illustrate Each Point

This is essential to the effectiveness of a Bible reading even more so than in the case of a textual sermon. As a rule, one should use Bible illustrations. There is an abundance of them, and they illustrate Bible truths far better than illustrations taken from books of stock illustrations.

E. He May Need to Limit the Subject

If his subject deals with a theme as large as "faith," for example, it is well to take up only a certain phase of it, rather than trying to cover the entire subject. Different aspects of faith may be presented: justifying faith; the faith that claims the promises; and so on.

For illustrative Bible readings, see pp. 147-155.

Chapter 13

GREAT CHAPTERS AS TEXTS

ONE IS OFTEN so much impressed with the truth as set forth completely and vividly in one chapter of the Bible that he desires to take that chapter as a text. This is a legitimate practice often honored with signal blessing and profit. Some of the greatest and most helpful sermons ever preached have had texts as large as an entire chapter.

Here are some suggestions in the use of such chapters:

I. ONE SHOULD CHOOSE A COMPLETE CHAPTER WHICH HAS IN IT A COMPLETE SUBJECT

I Corinthians 15 contains a complete subject: "The Resurrection of the Body." I Corinthians 13 is a complete treatise on the subject of "Love." John 17, "The Prayer of Our Lord," is also a complete subject. It would be very difficult to deal with some chapters in Proverbs and Psalms in this way.

II. HE SHOULD ASCERTAIN THE TRUE SETTING OF THE CHAPTER

It is useless to preach on Romans 8, for instance, unless one has in mind the preceding chapters. No exposition of this wonderful chapter would be complete that did not relate itself to the chapters preceding it. This is especially true of chapters chosen from the prophets. Their relation to the history and condition of the times must be considered before a sermon is prepared with the chapter as its text (cf. Isa. 6 with II Chron. 26). Sometimes the purpose of the entire book must be considered before one can arrive at a true understanding of the chapter.

III. HE MUST ANALYZE THE CHAPTER

The chapter should be outlined and divided, so he may know what its general divisions and subdivisions are. The American Standard Version will greatly help in this direction. He should read the chapter over carefully until the outline stands out bold and clear, keeping at it until he succeeds. As a rule the great chapters chosen as texts divide themselves naturally. For example, a careful reading of John 17 reveals three natural divisions of Christ's prayer which a careful reader could scarcely miss: for Himself, for His apostles, and for the future Church.

IV. HE MUST GET THE MAIN THEME OF THE CHAPTER

It may require many readings of the chapter to secure this result, but it must be done. Sermonizing is not easy work anyway. The theme of I Corinthians 13 is "Love"; chapter 14, "Spiritual Gifts"; chapter 15, "The Resurrection."

V. HE SHOULD SURROUND THE MAIN THEME WITH QUESTIONS

He can answer these questions from the contents of the chapter. If he takes I Corinthians 13, then he might ask, What is love? What are its characteristics? How does it manifest itself? What is its relation to and comparison with other gifts and graces of the Spirit? and so on. These answers will furnish him with the divisions and subdivisions of the chapter and also of his sermon. All his sermon will then be in his text. He will not be likely to wander from his text, which will then be a text in reality and not, as is often the case, a pretext.

VI. HE MIGHT ALSO COMPARE THE PARALLEL ACCOUNTS

This is especially true of chapters chosen from the Kings and Chronicles and sometimes the prophets. There are some passages in the Kings which have their sequel in the Chronicles and others in the prophets which have their sequel in some of the four books of Kings and Chronicles.

For illustrative sermons on Great Chapters as Texts, see pp. 156-158.

Chapter 14

ILLUSTRATIONS AND THEIR USE

I. THEIR IMPORTANCE

ONE NEED SCARCELY SPEAK of the great importance of the right use of illustrations in preaching. It is conceded on every side. The greatest preachers have been masters in the art of illustration. The pictorial satisfies an inherent desire on the part of an audience. Children love stories, and scarcely any man grows so old as not to enjoy a story. One of the leading Chicago papers pays its principal cartoonist more than twenty thousand dollars a year; many a reader has said that often the cartoon has been of more value than the rest of the paper. This was probably an exaggerated comparison, but it may illustrate the value of our subject.

Perhaps our Lord set forth by His example the value of illustrations in preaching more than anyone else did. His discourses abound in anecdotes, illustrations, and similes. No wonder the crowds hung for days upon His words as they fell from His lips. Pictorial and picturesque preaching will always get a hearing. The ability of any public speaker to turn the ears of his audience into eyes constitutes an essential element in his success. As the Apostle puts it, we are to "make all men see." It has been well said that "the eye is the pioneer of all learning." "Always throwing light upon the matter—that is the only part of the speech worth hearing," said Carlyle.

The work of the preacher is to make men first *see* things, then *feel* them, then *act* upon them. If the first result is not gained, the others will obviously not be obtained; whereas, if the first is gained, the other two often go along with it.

The use of illustrations is a great help to the audience to enable them to carry home the truth of the sermon. How many times we hear of people who have forgotten the text and the argument of the sermon, but who well remember the illustration used and invariably along with it the truth intended to be conveyed and fixed in the mind. Indeed, many an entire sermon, which otherwise would have been forgotten, has been recalled in its entirety by means of recalling an illustration used in the sermon. Just as scientists are said to be able to construct an entire animal from one bone, so many a whole sermon has been recalled by the use of one illustration.

Who has not noted the effect of an illustration upon an audience which was sleepy and listless? How quickly they prick up their ears when the preacher says, "Now let me illustrate this." How quickly every countenance is lighted up with an expectant expression! How alert is each mind! How entirely changed the complexion of the audience! The mere statement that a man is miserable who lays up treasure for himself and is not rich toward God might have been stated in ever so forcible language without reaching the conscience of the hearers. But our Lord proceeded to say, "The ground of a rich man brought forth plentifully," and so on, and closed with the words, "Thou fool, this night thy soul shall be required of thee. So is every one that is not rich toward God." Then no con-

science could remain unmoved, no hearer could any longer
be indifferent to the truth proclaimed. Our Lord's auditors
seem to have been so deeply moved, so intensely interested, so wholly absorbed in what He had to say that they
seem to have forgotten He was using mere illustrations.
At least once they interrupted Him and broke in upon one
of His parables with the declaration, "Lord, he hath ten
pounds!"

How keenly David's conscience was aroused by the story
of the little ewe lamb as told by Nathan the prophet!
How vividly Ezekiel portrayed the religious condition of
Israel by his use of such figures as scales, shears, razor,
knife, fire, tiles!

II. THE PURPOSE OF ILLUSTRATIONS

A. They Throw Light Upon the Subject

To "illustrate" means to light up, to give luster to, to
illuminate, to throw light upon, to make intelligible. Says
Cowper:

> The sense was dark—'twas therefore fit
> With simile to illustrate it.

An illustration is to the sermon what a window is to a
house—it lets light in. Illustrations are the windows of
speech—through them the truth shines. Logic may lay the
foundation and build the walls, but illustrations are the
windows to let the light in. No one would want to live in
a house without windows. So no one cares much about
listening to a sermon which contains no illustrations to
throw light upon the subject. "You have no 'likes' in your
sermons. Christ taught that the kingdom of heaven was
'like' leaven, 'like' a grain of mustardseed. You tell us
what things *are*, but you never tell us *what they are like.*"

Such was Dr. John Hall's criticism of a brother minister. In every age of the church's history, the most effective preachers have been those who have made judicious use of illustration in imitation of Christ's method of proclaiming the truth.

B. They Explain

Yet, to illustrate has a wider meaning than to throw light; it is used also to explain the subject. An illustration setting forth something similar or analogous to the case in hand will often make the subject plain. The power of the Holy Ghost which cannot be seen but may be felt can be helpfully explained by the illustration of the galvanic battery, the power of which one can feel but cannot see. "Many of Jesus' parables and pictures are more than mere illustrations; they have in them the imagination's power of interpretation, the revealing vision of the poet. The parable of the Pharisee and the Publican (Luke 18) is more than an illustrative example, it is, as Julicher classes it, 'an example of the spiritual worth of humility before God.' It reveals, as in a transparency, the essential and hidden evil of a religious class. Our Lord's controversy with the Pharisees sums itself up in this revealing picture where the inner spirit and tendency of Pharisaism is brought to a luminous point. The parable has the force of a revelation, suddenly illuminating a whole spiritual world. The same quality is in the illustrations of hypocrisy in Matthew 6. . . . Jesus takes the cases of almsgiving, prayer, fasting. . . . These were the fashionable religious virtues of the day, and therefore the chosen theatre of hypocrisy: self-seeking in religion leaves the humble sequestered virtues alone; and Christ's pictures of ostentatious service there, have that direct illumination of the religious and ethical imagination which sets it free from the bondage of all externalism. Many of the parables have this quality, such as the Seed Growing in Secret, the Good Samaritan, the Unmerciful Servant, the Prodigal Son, the Two Debtors."—See "Illustrations," *Dictionary of Christ and the Gospels.*

C. They Prove

Illustrations may be used for the purpose of proof. Especially is this true of illustrations from analogy. For example, in Romans 6 and 7 the Apostle uses three illustrations to show the absurdity of supposing that justification by faith will encourage sin. Believers are *dead* to sin and *risen* to another life; they have ceased to be the *slaves* of sin and have become *servants* unto holiness; they have ceased to be *married* to the law and have become united to a new husband to whom they must now bear fruit. Each one of these illustrations is not merely explanatory of the believer's position but involves the argument from analogy (cf. W. J. Bryan, *Christ Jesus' Proof of Immortality*).

D. They Give Ornamentation

One must be guarded in this use of illustration, always remembering the old saying, "We ornament construction and not construct ornament." That is, we use illustrations in order that we may make the style of our message more interesting, not merely ornamental. Some writer has well said: "Those whose style is barren of such ornament should seek after it, not by tying on worn and faded artificial flowers, but by encouraging the subject to blossom, if that be at all its nature." With this the preacher has little to do, for the cultivation of style is not his main purpose.

E. They Can Bring Conviction

An illustration may be used to arouse the conscience and clinch the truth. How grandly and vividly this use of illustration is exemplified in Nathan's dealings with David (II Sam. 12). The hammer of argument may drive home the nail of truth, but it takes the sledgehammer of illustration to efficiently clinch it.

III. THE SOURCES OF ILLUSTRATIONS

A. One Should Be On the Lookout for Illustrations Everywhere

He should seek to "find tongues in trees, books in running brooks; sermons in stones, and . . . [illustrations] in everything."

It is said Christ noticed many things in His days on earth. Note the words "He observed"—how the Pharisees chose the chief seats, how the people of His day did their marketing, dressed themselves, trained or mistrained their families, went to church for good or evil purposes, spoke hard words to or concerning one another. This is how Christ got His illustrations—He observed. He kept an open eye for them. The audience gave this great Preacher His illustrations, and what they gave Him He took and gave back to them. Christ drew his illustrations from the lilies, the raven, salt, a candle, a bushel, a long-faced hypocrite, gnats, moths, large gates and small gates, a needle's eye, yeast in bread, a mustard seed, a fishing net, debtors and creditors, and so on.

What a wonderful eye Jesus had for the suggestiveness of the material world! The falling of a sparrow to the ground, the growing of a lily, the sailing of a ship, the readiness of the fields for the harvest, the grinding of meal by women at the mill, the reddening glow of the evening sky—all these things were quickly caught up by Him and used in His sermons. The whole heaven and earth became to Him a picture gallery of illustrations. He saw the deepest truths illustrated in the world around Him. The star, the dewdrop, the flower, the field—all were ablaze with lustrous truth for Him.

Why should not we behold all these things which God has made: the sky, the star, the dewdrop, the lily, the sparrow? These all are here with us as they were with Him. Having eyes, let us see; having ears, let us hear. Let us not be content to find all our illustrations in musty, worn-out books of stock anecdotes when all around us nature is alive with illuminated and illustrative truth. The preacher who has wide-open eyes and ears will always be looking for things about him to which he can *liken* the truth he is seeking to present.

B. More Particular Sources of Illustrations Include:

1. Newspapers

These show how "our Father is ruling the world." Periodicals frequently print articles indicating the relation of world events to Bible teaching and prophecy.

2. History

One should study ancient, medieval, and modern history. It has a peculiar and almost unrivalled charm for illustrative purposes.

3. Poetry

This fruitful field should not be neglected. To be at home with the poets, one should read a good poem each day. He should classify it after having read it, so it will be ready for use at any time of need.

4. BIOGRAPHY

What a rich mine is to be found in this subject! How full of illustration is human life! Is not that the reason why the Old Testament is so interesting? It is so full of biography. How often Paul intersperses his discourses with little personal snatches from his own life. Everybody is interested in real life, in biography. Therefore, the preacher should read the lives of great explorers, great missionaries, great preachers, great men, great women.

5. THE SCIENCES, THE ARTS, AND THE INVENTIONS

These furnish rich material. Painting, sculpture, electricity, telegraphy, radium, astronomy, geology, architecture, music, chemistry, and so on—all are rich in illustrative material. Jesus made use of astronomy when He referred to the signs of the sun and the moon, the falling stars, the condition of the sky in the morning and in the evening. When He referred to the rocks, the mountains, and the stony places, did He not hint at geology? Even architecture did not escape Him, for He spoke of the two buildings, the one built on sand and the other on the rock. Music did not meet with a slight from the great Teacher, for He said, "We have piped unto you, and ye have not danced."

6. THE THREE KINGDOMS: ANIMAL, VEGETABLE, MINERAL.

Jesus spoke of wolves, sheep, goats, camels, insects, birds. He referred to the vine, vegetables, grain, seed, corn, wheat, tares, lilies. Pearls, gold, and salt were used by Him to set forth phases of truth. Scenes from domestic life were abundant in his discourses—wardrobe, banking, marriage, grinding, baking. In religious matters He referred to fasting, praying, tithing. In anatomy He spoke of the lips, heart, feeling, eyes, body, hands.

7. Children

These are an unfailing source of illustration. Christ likened the generation in which He lived "to children playing in the marketplace." The temper, habits, play, and disposition of children are instructive and may be found helpful in the illustration of certain phases of truth.

8. The Imagination

This must be carefully safeguarded. Within a limited sphere it may be drawn on as a fruitful source for making pictures. It is perfectly proper to invent an illustration, providing you let your audience know it is an invention and do not seek to palm it off on them as having a true fact for a basis. Such an illustration may be introduced with the words "It is as if," or "Suppose a case," or "Let us imagine."

9. Object Illustrations

A flower may be used to illustrate the resurrection; a magnet, the mysterious power of the Holy Spirit; a watch, the complex character of the human frame as it sets forth the wisdom of God; a blank book, how God keeps a record of our lives; an artificial flower, hypocrisy; a single thread easily broken but many threads being hard to break, the binding force of habit; an ordinary trap, the deceptiveness of temptation; the process of photography, the sensitiveness of the heart to good and evil influences.

IV. SUGGESTIONS AND CAUTIONS IN THE USE OF ILLUSTRATIONS

A. One Should Beware of Books of Stock Illustrations

The preacher should avoid the practice of feathering his arrows with illustrations from such books. The book of life and nature is open before him, from which he can make his own illustrations. Said the late Henry Ward Beecher: "Do you suppose I study old musty books when I want to preach? I study *you*. When I want to deliver a discourse on theology I study *you*. When I want to study more about the doctrine of depravity I study *you*. When I want to know what is right and what is wrong, I see how *you* do, and I have abundant illustrations on every side." Someone described the preaching of Beecher as follows: "He steps into a blacksmith's shop, and watches the sparks fly for a few minutes, then to his study and his pulpit to talk about 'the steel that has suffered most.' If the blacksmith were there, he understood all about the effect of life's discipline upon character—furnace, anvil, vise, the rasp, the emery, the hammer, were tools of which he knew well the operation. Beecher took his sermons and illustrations from life instead of from books. He put the repose of the granite hills, the smell of the new-mown hay, the lowing of the cattle, and the gambols of the lamb into them. Every sunset cloud effect he ever saw paid tribute to his sermons. The beggar was there, the student, the clerk in the store, and the waiter in the restaurant. He preached where people lived. He brought God down into the streets and workshops and homes of Brooklyn, a God full of sympathy for men's weaknesses and helpfulness for their daily trials!"

No sensible person casts any slur upon the use of illustrations in preaching. Men do complain sometimes, and rightly so, as to their source. Illustrations should be fresh, new, helpful, and gathered as the manna was—fresh every day. This is what an audience asks and has a right to expect. Held-over, stock illustrations soon run to seed like a pansy garden whose owner refuses to pluck the blossoms.

B. Illustrations Should Be Simple

How simple and easily understood were Christ's illustrations. Anyone, even a child, could understand them. The same should be said of the illustrations used today. It has been well said that the illustrations used in the average sermon "are so often cumbered with scientific learning and historic lore, so that like a stained glass window in a cathedral, however beautiful in pattern, they let in little light. But when Christ built up His discourses, doctrines were the pillars, and illustrations the open windows to flood the whole with sunshine."

C. They Should Be within the Comprehension of the Audience

This is more than can be said of many sermons and illustrations used in these days. Not long ago a young minister from one of our universities spent about ten minutes of the sermon time illustrating the doctrine he was inculcating by referring his audience—composed of farmers in a village far from a city of any size—to some latest discovery in science with which they had absolutely no acquaintance and of which they doubtless had never heard. The result was tedious in the extreme. The audience was listless, restless, and sleepy. However, when at the close of his sermon he referred them to the life-giving power that lay inherent in the seed, the restored and keen interest in this relevant illustration was very manifest.

The audience must understand the illustrations, which should therefore spring from their level, their memory, their experiences, their familiar observations. Illustrations drawn from a region remote from their actual life meet with no response. James Gordon Bennett once drew an editorial writer, who prided himself on writing for educated men, to the window of the *Herald* office, saying, "Do you see those people down there on Broadway?" "Yes," said the writer. "Well," declared Bennett, "I want you to write for those men down there." Let the preacher consider his audience and then talk to "those people." He should find his illustration where he can, but be sure it finds them. It will if he gets their viewpoint and sees what they are needing.

D. Lies Must Not Appear in Illustrations

Illustrations from the lives of other men must not be attributed to the preacher's own experience. That is lying, which does not bring glory to God.

E. One Must Never Make a Point for the Sake of Telling a Story

Such a practice may be admissible in an after-dinner speech, but is strictly out of place in a Gospel message. On being advised to use certain decorations, an architect declared it would violate the first rule of architecture. He replied. "We must never construct ornament, but only ornament construction."

F. The Illustration Must Illustrate

The preacher must ask himself, "Does this story or illustration throw light on the subject for me; does it help me to understand the subject better?" If it does not help him, it will not help his audience. If it throws light upon the matter for him, it very likely will for the people to whom he speaks. When one holds a light for another, it is usual for the one holding it to do it so he himself can see by it. It is also the rule for effective illustration. The illustration must not exclude the truth one is seeking to illustrate.

G. One Must Guard Against Too Many Illustrations

Usually one illustration for each point is sufficient. If two are used for one point there is danger that they may neutralize each other. A second illustration should be used only when the first has failed to do its proper work. This is sometimes necessary.

H. The Preacher Must Know His Illustration and Know How to Tell It

He should know his illustration as to its nature and its truth. Not long ago a preacher used the following simile as setting forth power of influence: "One drop of iodine will give a purple hue to a thousand gallons of water." A physician who was present took the preacher to task after the sermon for stating what was not true. Iodine, he claimed, had no such strength.

The preacher must know how to tell a story. Many a good illustration has been spoiled by poor telling. To be able to tell a story well and effectively is quite an art. Special attention must be paid to details. Here are some borrowed suggestions on good storytelling:

1. Seeing it

If one is to make others see it, he must see it himself.

One cannot make clear to others what is not perfectly clear to himself.

2. FEELING IT

If the preacher is not moved by the illustration, how can he expect to move others by its recital?

3. SHORTENING IT

Brevity is the soul of storytelling. Short stories are in demand by the pulpit as well as by the press. The probabilities are that the average illustration is too long.

4. EXPANDING IT

It may be very meager in the necessary background; it may be deficient in detail necessary for effective impression.

5. MASTERING IT

The preacher should practice it, repeating it so often that he can tell it without reference to his notes. Notes are fatal to the effectiveness of an illustration. He should repeat it often in private before he gives it in public.

6. REPEATING IT

Repetition is the mother of good storytelling. Do not be afraid of telling a good story many times. Even "twice-told tales" may be interesting.

I. He Must Have Something to Illustrate

Illustrations have been compared to the barbs that fix the arrow in the target. But barbs alone are useless. An archer would be poorly equipped if he had nothing in his quiver but arrowheads and feathers. For an illustration to be useful or effective, there must be something to illustrate. It is possible to make a sermon consist completely of stories. The sermons of some evangelists bear ample witness to this fact, for if the stories were to be extracted from their sermons there would be nothing left on which one could make an intelligent and legitimate appeal.

J. He Should File Away His Illustrations

He will need a scrapbook or filing index so that he may file away his illustrations according to the themes or subjects they throw light upon. He should also keep a record as to when and where he may have used them.

PART II

OUTLINES OF SERMONS, GOSPEL MESSAGES, AND BIBLE READINGS

TEXTUAL SERMONS

Theme: THE RESURRECTION OF JESUS CHRIST

Text:

"And that he was buried, and that he rose again the third day according to the scriptures" (I Cor. 15:3).

"To whom also he shewed himself alive after his passion by many infallible proofs, being seen of them forty days, and speaking of the things pertaining to the kingdom of God" (Acts 1:3).

Introduction:

The important place of the doctrine in the Christian system

Body:

    I. THE NATURE OF THE RESURRECTION OF JESUS CHRIST

    Answering the question, What?

    A. The meaning of credibility

    B. The meaning of Christ's resurrection
      Negatively:
      1. Not a swoon
      2. Not a resuscitation
      3. Not continued existence of only the soul of Jesus

      Positively:

      A literal resurrection of the physical body of Jesus Christ from the tomb in Joseph's garden

II. The Proof of the Resurrection of Jesus Christ

Answering the question, Why?

A. Cause and effect:
   Here are certain effects, the causes for which can
   be traced only to the fact of Christ's resurrection.
   1. The empty tomb
   2. The Lord's day
   3. The Christian Church
   4. The New Testament

B. Testimony:
   1. The number of witnesses
   2. The credibility of the witnesses
   3. The nature of the fact witnessed
   4. The lack of motive for perjury

C. Experience: (I Cor. 15:17)
   1. Paul's
   2. Corinthians'
   3. Ours

III. The Necessity for the Resurrection of Jesus
Christ

Also answering, Why? but from another viewpoint

A. The sinlessness of His life, making it impossible
   that He should be held by death (Acts 2:24)
B. The vindication of the truth of all His claims
   (John 2:19; Matt. 12:38-40)
C. The sign of God's approval (Acts 2:23-24, 31-33)
D. To show God had accepted Christ's redemptive
   work in our behalf (Rom. 4:23-25)

IV. The Results of Jesus Christ's Resurrection

Answering the question, What then?

A. With reference to Christ Himself:
  1. It marked Him off as the Son of God in a unique sense (Rom. 1:4).
  2. It was the seal of the divine approval upon all His claims (Acts 2:23-24).

B. With reference to the believer:
  1. Assures him of his acceptance with God (Rom. 4:25).
  2. Assures him of all needed power (Eph. 1: 19-22).
  3. Grants to him the Holy Ghost (John 7:37-39; Acts 2:33).
  4. Is a guarantee of his own resurrection and immortality (II Cor. 4:14; John 14:19).

C. With reference to the world of men:
  1. Guarantees the resurrection of all men (I Cor. 15:22).
  2. Assures them of the certainty of a coming judgment (Acts 17:31).

Conclusion

———

Theme: THE NEW BIRTH

Text:

"Jesus answered and said unto him, Verily, verily, I say unto thee, Except a man be born again, he cannot see the kingdom of God. Nicodemus saith unto him, How can a man be born when he is old? can he enter the second time into his mother's

womb, and be born? Jesus answered, Verily, verily, I say unto
thee, Except a man be born of water and of the Spirit, he cannot enter into the kingdom of God. That which is born of the
flesh is flesh; and that which is born of the Spirit is spirit.
Marvel not that I said unto thee, Ye must be born again" (John
3:3-7).

Introduction:

The popular talk concerning the kingdom and how to
enter into it, introduced by John the Baptist's ministry

Body:

I. The New Birth Defined

    A. Negatively:
       1. Not baptism (Gal. 6:15; I Cor. 1:17)
       2. Not reformation (John 3:6; Titus 3:5)

    B. Positively:
       1. A birth from above, a spiritual coming to life
         (John 3:3-5; II Cor. 5:17)
       2. The impartation of the divine nature (II Peter
         1:4)
       3. A new and divine impulse (I John 3:6-9)

II. The Necessity of the New Birth

    A. Universal (John 3:3-5)

    B. Sinful condition of man demanding it (John
       3:6)

    C. Jesus declaring it to be absolutely necessary
       (John 3:5-7)

    D. The holiness of God demanding it (Heb. 12:14)

III. How the New Birth Takes Place

    A. The divine side:
       The work of God the Holy Spirit (John 1:12-13; 3:5; Titus 3:5)

    B. The human side:
      1. The acceptance of the Gospel message (James 1:18; I Peter 1:23; I Cor. 4:15)
      2. The personal acceptance of Jesus Christ (John 1:12; Gal. 3:26)

IV. The Results of the New Birth

    A. Godlikeness (Col. 3:10; Eph. 4:24)
    B. Victory over sin (I John 5:4; 3:9)
    C. Righteous living (I John 2:29)
    D. Love toward the brethren (I John 4:7)

Conclusion:

Have you been born again? If not, what then?

Theme: SPIRITUAL POWER

Text:

"But ye shall receive power, after that the Holy Ghost is come upon you: and ye shall be witnesses unto me both in Jerusalem, and in all Judaea, and in Samaria, and unto the uttermost part of the earth" (Acts 1:8).

Introduction

Body:

    I. What is Meant by Spiritual Power?

      What?

A. Negatively:

Not personal magnetism, eloquence, learning; not a human attainment.

B. Positively:

A divine gift—the possession of the Spirit of of power (The Greek word for "power" is "dynamite.")

II. THE EVIDENCES OF THE NEED OF SPIRITUAL POWER

Why?

A. The sad condition of the Church

B. The defeated Christian lives, as shown in
   1. Lack of victory over sin
   2. Lack of testimony for Christ
   3. Lack of influence for Christ

III. HOW TO GET SPIRITUAL POWER

How?

A. Earnestly desire it.

B. Put away sin.

C. Enthrone Christ.

D. Obey the Spirit.

E. Accept it by faith.

IV. THE RESULTS OF HAVING SPIRITUAL POWER

What then?

A. Victory over sinful self

B. Boldness in testimony

C. Transfigured and influential life

D. A revived Church

Conclusion

_____

Theme: FIRST LOVE LOST

Text:
"Nevertheless I have somewhat against thee, because thou hast left thy first love" (Rev. 2:4).

Introduction:
Christ's method of dealing with His Church

Body:

    I. What is First Love?

        A. The love of espousal or engagement (Jer. 2:2)

        B. The love of the new convert

    II. The Necessity of Keeping First Love

        A. Without it orthodoxy and service are nothing.

        B. No church has a right to exist without it (Rev. 2:5).

        C. Without love all is lost (I Cor. 13).

    III. Signs of Lost Love

        A. Not necessarily:
            1. Lack of activity (Rev. 2:2)
            2. Lack of orthodoxy (Rev. 2:2)
            3. Lack of patient suffering for Christ (Rev. 2:3)

        B. But definitely shown by the absence of:
            1. Personal love in service
            2. Joy in our activity for Christ
            3. Unselfishness and forgetfulness of self

IV. How First Love is Lost

    A. By neglecting to maintain fellowship and communion with God through the reading of the Word of God, prayer, and obedience

    B. By spiritual pride, forgetting unworthiness is still as great as at the time of conversion

V. How to Regain Lost Love

    A. Remember—your past experience, the atmosphere in which you once lived, and so on.

    B. Repent—turn back, confess, promise reformation.

    C. Return—do the first works over again.

Conclusion

Theme: A GREAT SALVATION—ITS REJECTION AND PENALTY

Text:

"How shall we escape, if we neglect so great salvation; which at the first began to be spoken by the Lord, and was confirmed unto us by them that heard him" (Heb. 2:3).

Introduction:

The preeminence of Christianity over Judaism

Body:

I. The Salvation Offered

    A. Its meaning—what?

    B. Great—how and why?
       1. Because of its Author—the Trinity engaged
          in its work
       2. Because of what it can do (v. 4)
       3. Because of the nature of the divine and
          human proofs submitted for its genuineness
          (v. 4)

II. THE ATTITUDE OF NEGLECT DESCRIBED

    A. Refusing to give heed (v. 1)

    B. Allowing to drift by (v. 1)

    C. Refusing to accept the well attested truth (vv. 3-4)

    D. Simply doing nothing—letting things slip (v. 1)

III. THE PENALTY VISITED

    A. Certain (vv. 2-3; cf. 12:25-29)

    B. Just (2:2)

    C. Commensurate with privileges (vv. 2-3)

    D. Described (10:26-29)

Conclusion:

Illustration showing danger and fatal consequences of neglect

———

Theme: THE NATURAL SOURCES OF RETRIBUTION

Text:

"We are verily guilty concerning our brother, in that we saw the anguish of his soul, when he besought us, and we would not hear; therefore is this distress come upon us" (Gen. 42:21).

Introduction:

No one text of Scripture contains such a complete survey of the inner sources of human penalty for sin. Nothing is said of any external accusation. Joseph's brethren do not yet know it is Joseph before whom they stand. No voice from Heaven reproaches them. Outside their own company, there do not appear to have been any witnesses of their dastardly outrage against their brother's liberty and their father's peace. "They said one to another," as by a simultaneous working of the retributive law in their own breasts, "We are verily guilty," and so on.

It is to be noted here that all the factors unite that enter into natural penalty. This makes the mission of this text the more obvious and impressive.

Body:

    I. Memory: "We saw the anguish of his soul."

        A. The recalling power of memory (twenty years recalled).

        B. The minuteness of detail: "He besought us," and so on.

        C. The peculiar persistence of memory; effort to forget only deepens impression.

    II. Conscience: "We are verily guilty."

Conscience is a compound faculty, the result of the joint working of a sense of rightness and a judgment of right and wrong.

        A. The sense of obligation always follows the judgment.

  B. Conscience is a whole court in itself: judge, jury, witnesses, sheriff, and so on.

  C. Remorse is its merciless sheriff and executioner.

III. REASON: "Therefore is this distress come upon us."

Here the punishment, as the logical outcome and reasonable penalty of the crime, is justified.

  A. Reason is a faculty which inquires as to the reason of things.

  B. It instinctively justifies a deserved punishment.

  C. It will ultimately vindicate the just judgment of God.

Conclusion:

In the persistent attempts to evade the plain Scriptural doctrine of retribution, men are resisting not only the teaching of revelation but also the testimony of their own inner life. Were there no divine penalties attached to evil doing, man has in himself, as the Latins used to say, "Index, judex, vindex."

             —A. T. PIERSON

Theme: CHRIST'S FOURFOLD WORK

Text:

"Who of God is made unto us wisdom, and righteousness, and sanctification, and redemption" (I Cor. 1:30).

Introduction:

This is the only text that in four consecutive leading words presents the complete view of Christ's redemptive work. It reminds us of the first time in which the four cardinal points of the compass are emphasized in Scripture, when Abraham was led by God to separate from Lot, letting his nephew have the best of the land. Here it seems that God says to the disciple who for holiness' sake separates himself from sin unto God, "Lift up your eyes and look north, south, east, and west; for all the land which you see, to you will I give it, and to your seed forever."

Here are the cardinal points in the spiritual landscape, and they take in the whole horizon of Christ's work for our salvation. Without Christ's work, we should neither know ourselves nor God. The *order* again is inviolable.

Body:

 I. Wisdom

  A. By correcting our errors of opinion and practice
  B. By confirming what is right and good
  C. By revealing what has up to now been unknown

 II. Righteousness

  A. By His own perfect obedience to the law
  B. By His vicarious and justifying death for sin
  C. By His intercession at God's right hand

 III. Sanctification

  A. By His perfect example of holiness
  B. By regeneration, imparting the new nature
  C. By the gift of the indwelling Spirit of holiness

 IV. Redemption

  A. By resurrection of the body: redemption of the body

    B. By final and full deliverance from sin: redemption of the spirit.

    C. By ushering us, body and spirit, into the heavenly home

—A. T. Pierson

Theme: THE FOURFOLD USE OF SCRIPTURE

Text:

"All scripture is given by inspiration of God, and is profitable for doctrine, for reproof, for correction, for instruction in righteousness" (II Tim. 3:16).

Introduction:

Here again four consecutive words embrace the whole realm of Scripture profit, and again the order is a part of the inspiration.

Body:

    I. Doctrine

The word means teaching. It covers the same ground as "wisdom" in the preceding outline of Christ's work. As a teacher He

    A. Corrects our errors (cf. Matt. 5:21-48).

    B. Confirms our right convictions.

    C. Reveals new truths.

    II. Reproof

This word seems to refer to the work on the *conscience,* as the preceding outline has to do with the understanding.

    A. Compelling the consciousness of sin and guilt

  B. Bringing us before the court of conscience
   (Rom. 2:15)

  C. Constraining to a new rectitude

III. Correction

This is not an easy word to render. It seems to carry
the idea of reconstruction—setting up fallen man on his
feet, restoring him.

  A. Discovering the only true foundation (Luke
   6:48)

  B. Building character and conduct with right material

  C. Out of ruins constructing a temple of God

IV. Instruction

Instruction in righteousness. This is teaching, like the
first, but it belongs not to the initial but to the advanced
stage. It is the teaching that fully equips for duty and
service.

  A. It is knowledge of the mysteries of God.

  B. It is the knowledge of the secrets of spiritual
   power.

  C. It is the full furnishing for service.

—A. T. Pierson

**Theme: THE GAIN OF THE WORLD AND THE
LOSS OF THE SOUL**

Text:

 "For what shall it profit a man, if he shall gain the whole
world, and lose his own soul? Or what shall a man give in exchange for his soul?" (Mark 8:36-37).

Introduction:

We should be careful to note the two things here contrasted. It does not necessarily mean the gaining of the present and the loss of the future, for those who lose the future do not necessarily get the most out of the present. Nor does it mean that in order to gain the future we must lose the present—for those who gain the future really get the best out of this life, too.

Body:

   I. What is the World That is Gained and the Soul That is Lost?

     A. The World (I John 2:15-17)

Everything in the world appeals to the senses: "the lust of the flesh, and the lust of the eyes, and the pride of life." To gain the world means to get all it has to give along these lines.

     B. The Soul (Luke 9:25—the man "himself")

The inner, real manhood and womanhood. To lose the soul means to lose oneself.

   II. Every Person Has a Soul of Infinite Value.

     A. The existence of the soul (Gen. 2:7)

     B. The value of the soul:
       1. Because of its divine origin
       2. Because of the price paid for its redemption
       3. Because of the great contention for its possession
       4. Because of the eternal destiny awaiting it

III. There Is Great Danger of Losing the Soul.

    A. There is a sense in which it is already lost.

    B. But there is a final loss that takes place in the future.

    C. The soul may be lost by trying to gain the world.
       1. A supposed gain: "if"
       2. An uncertain gain (cf. Luke 12:20)
       3. A difficult gain (cf. I Tim. 6:10)
       4. An unsatisfactory gain (cf. Eccles. 1 and 2)

    D. The loss of the soul is permanent and irretrievable. No exchange can save it when once its doom has been pronounced.

Conclusion:

This text invites you to picture yourself at the judgment bar of God, hearing the sentence of doom pronounced upon you. Then ask yourself the question of this text: "What shall it have profited me, gaining as I did the whole world, seeing I have now lost my soul, for which loss there is no exchange, no redemption?"

(It might be well to close with a striking illustration.)

Theme: THE RICH PUBLICAN OF JERICHO FOUND

Text:

"This day is salvation come to this house" (Luke 19:9).

Introduction

Body:

I. Hindrances

    A. Popular difficulty—a publican

    B. Moral difficulty—a sinner

    C. Business difficulty—rich

II. Aids

    A. A desire to see Jesus

    B. An effort to see Jesus

    C. Willingness to obey Jesus

III. Results

    A. A great confession

    B. A great restitution

    C. A great truth heralded (v. 10)

Conclusion

—Homiletic Review

EXPOSITORY SERMONS

Theme: A FOURFOLD ATTITUDE TOWARD SIN

Text:

"But if we walk in the light, as he is in the light, we have fellowship one with another, and the blood of Jesus Christ his Son cleanseth us from all sin. If we say that we have no sin, we deceive ourselves, and the truth is not in us. If we confess our sins, he is faithful and just to forgive us our sins, and to cleanse us from all unrighteousness. If we say that we have not sinned, we make him a liar, and his word is not in us. My little children, these things write I unto you, that ye sin not. And if any man sin, we have an advocate with the Father, Jesus Christ the righteous: And he is the propitiation for our sins: and not for ours only, but also for the sins of the whole world" (I John 1:7—2:2).

Introduction

Body:

    I. DENYING IT (1:8-10)

        A. Nature of the denial:
           1. As to the possession of a sinful nature (v. 8)
           2. As to the committal of sinful acts (v. 10)
        B. What is involved in such denial
           1. Self-deception (v. 8)
           2. Challenging God's statement (v. 7)
           3. Making God a liar (v. 10)
           4. The Word of God, as a norm, having no abiding place in the heart (v. 10)

II. CONFESSING IT (1:9)

A. The nature of confession
1. Confess—take sides with God against it. Admit it.
2. Renounce—forsake what you would have God remit.
3. Believe in the efficacy of the blood of Christ (vv. 7-9).
4. Accept God's declaration of forgiveness, based on His righteousness and justice (v. 9).

B. The result of confession
1. We are forgiven (v. 9).
2. We are cleansed from sin's guilt (v. 7) and sin's power (v. 9).

III. VICTORY OVER IT (2:1; cf. 1:7, 9)

A. Victory possible (2:1)

B. Its method
1. Word of God (2:14)
2. Divine nature (3:9)
3. Indwelling Holy Spirit (4:4)

IV. REPEATING IT OR FALLING INTO IT (1:7—2:2)

A. Admit that we do sin (2:1).

B. What to do when we sin
1. Recognize advocacy (2:1-2).
2. Recognize provision made for it (1:7-9; 2:2).
3. Confess it (see II above).

Conclusion

Theme: THE BELIEVER'S WALK

Text:

"For this cause we also, since the day we heard it, do not cease to pray for you, and to desire that ye might be filled with the knowledge of his will in all wisdom and spiritual understanding; That ye might walk worthy of the Lord unto all pleasing, being fruitful in every good work, and increasing in the knowledge of God; Strengthened with all might, according to his glorious power, unto all patience and longsuffering with joyfulness; Giving thanks unto the Father, which hath made us meet to be partakers of the inheritance of the saints in light" (Col. 1:9-12).

Introduction

Body:

    I. THE NATURE OF THE WALK

        A. Worthy of the Lord (v. 10)

        B. According to the revealed will of God (v. 9)

    II. THE MOTIVE OF THE WALK

        Unto the Lord Himself (v. 10)

    III. THE MEANS OF THE WALK

        A. Faith in Christ—the beginning (v. 4)

        B. Prayer—the continuation (v. 9)

        C. The Word of God—source of knowledge of God's will (v. 9)

        D. The indwelling Spirit of God (v. 4)

    IV. THE RESULTS OF THE WALK

        A. Well pleasing to God (v. 10)

    B. Fruitful in every good work (v. 10)

    C. An increasing knowledge of God (v. 10)

    D. Spiritual graces: patience, long-suffering, joy, thankfulness (vv. 11-12)

    E. An inheritance with the saints in light (v. 12)

Conclusion

Theme: THE DEATH OF JESUS CHRIST

Text:

"For when we were yet without strength, in due time Christ died for the ungodly. For scarcely for a righteous man will one die: yet peradventure for a good man some would even dare to die. But God commendeth his love toward us, in that, while we were yet sinners, Christ died for us. Much more then, being now justified by his blood, we shall be saved from wrath through him. For if, when we were enemies, we were reconciled to God by the death of his Son, much more, being reconciled, we shall be saved by his life. And not only so, but we also joy in God through our Lord Jesus Christ, by whom we have now received the atonement" (Rom. 5:6-11).

Introduction:

Its place in Pauline teaching

Body:

    I. SOMEONE DIED.

        A. This is an ordinary fact.

        B. Yet it is an extraordinary fact when we remember

            1. The character of the One who died.

            2. He could have avoided death.

            3. The claims associated with His death.

II. The People for Whom Christ Died

A. Sinners, ungodly, weak, enemies

B. Meaning of the words "died for them"

III. The Purpose of Christ's Death

A. Negatively: Not to induce God to love men

B. Positively: That man might be changed
   1. Justified
   2. Reconciled
   3. Saved from wrath
   4. Saved by His life

Conclusion:

Do we unheedingly pass that Cross? Is it nothing to us? What interest do we have in that death?

BIBLE READINGS

Theme: PEACE

This Bible reading on "Peace," while having far too much material for one address, nevertheless affords a fine illustration as to the untold wealth of Bible truth that can be obtained with the aid of the concordance (Strong's or Young's) and the Bible.

I. THE MEANING OF PEACE

A. The Greek word appears to mean "to bind" (*eirēnē*, from *eirō*), implying severance and union.

B. The English word implies a *pact*, compact, an agreement (*paciscor*).

C. The Hebrew word implies the ideas of friendliness, rest, security, *completeness* (*shălōm*).

N. B.—Note the order of experience: union; agreement; friendship; rest; security; completeness.

II. THE NEED OF PEACE

A. Peace of conscience in pardon and acceptance (Isa. 48:22; Rom. 3:17; Ps. 120:6)

B. Peace of heart in rest and fellowship (Num. 6:26; 25:12; Ps. 4:8; 29:11).

III. THE PROVISION OF PEACE

A. "Peace with God" (Rom. 5:1) means barriers are removed.

B. "The peace of God" (Phil. 4:7) means burdens are relieved.

N. B.—These are distinguished in John 20:19 and 21 (see context); also, in John 14:27 peace is a *legacy* and a *gift*.

IV. The Source of Peace

A. "Of God" (Phil 4:7; Col. 3:15 [cf. A.S.V.])
B. "The God of peace" (Rom. 15:33; 16:20; I Cor. 14:33; II Cor. 13:11; Phil. 4:9; I Thess. 5:23; Heb. 13:20).

V. The Medium of Peace

A. Christ's person (Eph. 2:14, *autos*; Isa. 9:6, Prince; II Thess. 3:16, *Kurios*; Heb. 7:2, *basileus*)
B. Christ's work (Eph. 2:15, *poiōv*; Col. 1:20, *eirēnopoiēsas* Cf. Isa. 53:5)
C. Christ's preaching (Eph. 2:17; Acts 10:36)
D. Christ's gift (John 14:27)

VI. The Sphere of Peace

A. In Christ (John 16:33)
B. In the Holy Spirit (Rom. 14:17)

VII. The Instrumentality of Peace

A. The Gospel (Eph. 6:15; I Cor. 7:15; Luke 1:79)
B. Faith (Rom. 5:1; 15:13)
C. The mind of the Spirit (Rom. 8:6)

VIII. THE CHARACTERISTICS OF PEACE

    A. Great (Ps. 119:165; cf. Isa. 48:18, "as a river")

    B. Abundant (Ps. 37:11; 72:7; cf. I Pet. 1:2 and Jude 2, *piēthuntheiē*)

    C. Indescribable (Phil. 4:7)

    D. Perfect (Isa. 26:3)

    E. Everlasting (Isa. 9:7, "no end")

IX. THE POWER OF PEACE

    A. To fill (Rom. 15:13)

    B. To guard (Phil. 4:7)

    C. To rule (Col. 3:15, *brabeuetō*, "to umpire")

X. THE COMPANIONS OF PEACE

    A. Grace (Rom. 1:7)

    B. Mercy (Gal. 6:16)

    C. Righteousness (Rom. 14:17)

    D. Joy (Rom. 15:13)

    E. Faith (II Tim. 2:22)

    F. Love (II Cor. 13:11)

    G. Life (Rom. 8:6)

    H. Holiness (Heb. 12:14)

    I. Purity (James 3:17)

    J. Gentleness (James 3:17)

XI. THE OUTCOME OF PEACE

    A. In character (Gal. 5:22, "fruit . . . peace")

    B. In fellowship (Eph. 4:3, "bond of peace"; Eph. 6:23, cf. *eirēneuein* in Mark 9:50; Rom. 12:18; II Cor. 13:11; I Thess. 5:13)

C. In action (Matt. 5:9, *eirēnopoios*; James 3:17, *eirēnikos*)

D. In service (Eph. 6:15 *etoimasia eirēnēs*)

XII. The Possibilities of Peace

A. Through life (Mark 5:34, *hupage eis eirēnēn*; Luke 7:50, *poreuou eis*)

B. At death (Luke 2:29, *apolueis en eirēnē*)

C. In eternity (II Peter 3:14, *autō eurethēnai en eirēnē*)

XIII. The Scope of Peace

A. On earth (Luke 2:14)

B. In Heaven (Luke 19:38)

XIV. The Secret of Peace

A. Surrender (Isa. 9:7, "*government* and peace"; II Thess. 3:16, "*Lord* of peace")

B. Trust (Isa. 26:3; Rom. 15:13)

C. Obedience (Ps. 119:165; Isa. 32:17; James 3:18)

D. Earnestness (I Peter 3:11, *zētē satō kai diōxatō*; Heb. 12:14, *diōkete*)

We can easily understand from all this the imperative necessity of realizing at once and continually the things that belong to our peace (Luke 19:42), and then of pursuing the things of peace (Rom. 14:17).—*Record of Christian Work*

Theme: CHRIST SUFFERING FOR US

After all the passages in the Bible treating on this subject have been looked up and classified and a general knowledge of the subject obtained, it will be found there are more passages than can be used in one Bible reading. One should sift them, choosing the best. The following may be the result for us:

I. Being brought to God: a new access (I Peter 3:18)

II. Dying to sin and passing into life: a new death (I Peter 2:24)

III. Being made the righteousness of God in Him: a new spirit (II Cor. 5:21)

IV. Receiving the promise of the Spirit through faith: the newness of the Spirit (Gal. 3:13)

V. Being given an example: a new example (I Peter 2:21)

VI. Being redeemed from all iniquity: a new redemption (Titus 2:14)

VII. Being delivered from this evil world: a new deliverance (Gal. 1:4)

VIII. Living together with Him: a new fellowship (I Thess. 5:10)

It will thus be seen there are eight intents and results of Christ's vicarious death.

———

Theme: THE WATER OF LIFE

I. ITS CHARACTER

A. Living (John 4:10)

B. Clear (Rev. 22:1)

C. Pure (Rev. 22:1)

    D. Abundant (Ezek. 47:1-9)
    E. Free (Rev. 21:6)

II. For Whom Provided?
    A. The thirsty (Rev. 21:6)
    B. Whosoever (Rev. 22:17)

III. The Way to Obtain It
    A. Come (Rev. 22:17)
    B. Take (Rev. 22:17)

Theme: REDEMPTION

I. What I Am Redeemed With
    A. Blood (I Peter 1:19)
    B. Power (Neh. 1:10)

II. What I Am Redeemed From
    A. Bondage (Exodus 6:6)
    B. Enemy (Ps. 106:10)
    C. Iniquity (Titus 2:14)
    D. Curse of the law (Gal. 3:10)

III. What the Lord Has Redeemed
    A. The soul (Ps. 49:8)
    B. The body (Rom. 8:23)
    C. The life (Ps. 103:4)

IV. The Beauty of the Redemption
    A. Plenteous (Ps. 130:7)
    B. Precious (Ps. 49:8)
    C. Eternal (Heb. 9:12)

Theme: THE LOVE OF GOD
 I. Infinite in its character (John 17:23-24)
 II. Constraining in its power (II Cor. 5:14)
 III. Inseparable in its object (Rom. 8:35-37)
 IV. Individual in its choice (Gal. 2:20)
 V. Universal in its extent (John 3:16)
 VI. Unchanging in its purpose (John 13:1)
 VII. Everlasting in its duration (Jer. 31:3)

Theme: JUSTIFICATION
 I. What it is (Rom. 4:5-8)
 II. Who justifies (Rom. 8:33)
 III. Who is justified (Rom. 3:24; 5:9)
 IV. From what we are justified (Acts 13:39)
 V. Result of being justified (Rom. 5:1)

Theme: REPENTANCE
 I. What it is (Matt. 21:29)
 II. Its source (II Tim. 2:25)
 III. Its necessity (Acts 8:22)
 IV. Its results (Luke 15:7; 17:3)
 V. By whom commanded (Acts 17:30)
 VI. In whose name (Luke 24:47)

—CHARLES INGLIS

Theme: STANDING OF MAN BEFORE GOD

I. APART FROM CHRIST

A. Past
1. Created in image of God (Gen. 1:26-27)
2. Sin entered, and death by sin (Rom. 5:12)

B. Present
1. All under sin (Rom. 3:9)
2. None righteous (Rom. 3:10-12)
3. Judgment resting on all (Rom. 3:19)
4. All under curse (Gal. 3:10)

C. Future
1. Wrath abideth (John 3:36)
2. And the unbelieving shall have their part in the lake that burns forever (Rev. 21:8)

II. UNITED WITH CHRIST

A. Past
1. Predestined according to His purpose (Eph. 1:11

B. Present
1. Perfected forever (Heb. 10:14)
2. Righteous (II Cor. 5:21)
3. No condemnation (Rom. 8:1)
4. Redeemed from curse (Gal. 3:13)

C. Future
1. Forever with Him (John 14:3)
2. Heirs of God (Rom. 8:17)

—R. S. BEAL

Theme: SEVEN INDISPENSABLE THINGS

    I. Without shedding of blood there is no remission of sins (Heb. 9:22).

   II. Without faith it is impossible to please God (Heb. 11:6).

  III. Without works faith is dead (James 2:26).

  IV. Without holiness no man shall see the Lord (Heb. 12:14).

    V. Without love I am nothing (I Cor. 13:1-3).

  VI. Without chastisement you are not sons (Heb. 12:8).

 VII. Without Jesus Christ you can do nothing (John 15:5).

GREAT CHAPTERS AS TEXTS

JOHN XVII

In the first place, note that this chapter contains one great theme: "The High-priestly Prayer of our Lord." Note again that its setting places it in the last week, indeed, within the last day or so before our Lord's crucifixion. Further, a careful reading of the chapter reveals the three-fold analysis. There are no parallel accounts.

Theme: THE HIGH-PRIESTLY PRAYER OF OUR LORD

Text:
John 17:1-26

Introduction:
The important place that prayer, particularly intercessory prayer, occupied in the life of our Lord

Body:

I. OUR LORD'S PRAYER FOR HIS OWN GLORIFICATION (vv. 1-5)

A. By enduring the Cross (v. 1, "the hour")

B. By blessing humanity (v. 2, "give eternal life")

C. By perfect obedience (vv. 3-5, "finished the work")

156

II. OUR LORD'S PRAYER FOR HIS DISCIPLES (vv. 6-19)

    A. Their relation to the Father and the Son described (vv. 6-8)

    B. Prayer for their unity (v. 11)

    C. Prayer for their preservation from the evil one (vv. 11-16)

    D. Prayer for their separation unto service (vv. 17-19)

III. OUR LORD'S PRAYER FOR THE FUTURE CHURCH (vv. 20-26)

    A. For its unity (vv. 21-23)

    B. For its power and testimony before the world (vv. 21-23)

    C. That the whole Church may be gathered ultimately with Him in glory (vv. 24-26)

Conclusion:

The strength and inspiration which come from the consciousness that our High Priest is thus praying for us

---

ISAIAH I

Because it presents us with a completed theme, this chapter may well be chosen as a text for a sermon. A careful reading of the chapter reveals to us the theme: "God's Controversy with His People Israel." The scene is that of a court trial. God is the Judge and Plaintiff; the prophet is the witness; the people of Israel, the defendants; the charge is clearly stated, and the verdict announced.

Theme: GOD'S CONTROVERSY WITH HIS PEOPLE ISRAEL

Text:

Isaiah 1

Introduction:

The moral and spiritual condition of the nation at this time

Body:

I. God's Complaint Against His People (vv. 1-3)

A. Disobedience (vv. 2-3)

B. Rebellion (vv. 2-3, "rebelled against me")

C. Ingratitude (v. 3, "my people doth not consider")

II. The Prophet as a Witness Reinforcing God's Indictment (vv. 4-9)

A. Showing the course of sin (v. 4)

B. Showing the punishment for sin (vv. 5-9)

III. The People's Plea of Defense (vv. 11-14)

A. Laborious sacrifices (vv. 11-12)

B. Much ceremonialism (vv. 13-14)

IV. The Conclusion or Summing Up of the Trial (vv. 16-31)

A. The call to repentance and reason (vv. 16-18)

B. The verdict and sentence announced (vv. 19-20)

C. How the sentence will work out (vv. 21-31)

Moody Press, a ministry of the Moody Bible Institute, is designed for education, evangelization and edification. If we may assist you in knowing more about Christ and the Christian life, please write us without obligation to: Moody Press, c/o MLM, Chicago, Illinois 60610.